STEPPING UP!

STEPPING UP!

Discover the *Power* of Your Position

Johnny McGowan

Foreword by Joel Osteen

[signature]
3/25/19

FaithWords

New York • Nashville

Contents

To Margrett McGowan, my mother

As the old saying goes, more is caught than taught. I saw my mom live in such a way that she never knew a stranger, always sharing her continuous smile and abiding joy. Her impact on my life remains second to none. Writing this book is one of my life's greatest achievements, and I know she is celebrating in heaven with me, smiling her trademark smile. I miss and love her dearly.

Foreword by Joel Osteen

Jesus said that if you want to be great in the kingdom, if you want to live a blessed life, there's a simple key: You have to serve other people. He wasn't talking about an event that happens every once in a while. He was talking about a lifestyle in which you live to help others. When you live a "serve others" lifestyle, you help friends, you volunteer in your community, and you take care of loved ones. It becomes a part of who you are. You develop an attitude of giving toward everyone you meet. The more willing you are to serve others, the higher God can take you.

God may be seeking to bless you in ways that you never thought possible or in ways that you don't expect. A servant in the eyes of others is a leader in the eyes of God, and faithfully serving others is the means by which God intends for you to gain the knowledge and insight that you will later use to fulfill your own purpose and destiny.

I can think of no one better to write this book than Johnny McGowan. I have known Johnny for almost forty years, and throughout that time he has served not only our family and our church but countless others as well. He has always proven faithful, dependable, and trustworthy, and he is one of the greatest servant leaders I know.

As one who understands what it means to find purpose through service, Johnny shares with you how your destiny can be realized when you are willing to serve others—whether it is through your job, by being a good neighbor, or by taking up a cause that helps people. He explains that when you are willing to step up and do the right thing, the best way that you know how, you establish yourself firmly in God's plan for your life. If you trust God when He asks you to serve another and give it your best effort, God's blessings will begin to flow into your life and through everything you do.

Johnny is living proof that God can do great things through the heart of a servant. I urge you to read this book and embrace the ideas and encouragement you'll find on every page. If you allow them to take hold and commit yourself to stepping up, you will soon step into the power and abundance that God intended for you to have in your life.

Introduction

True service for sustained success is never about instant gratification. To have a servant's heart is to know that you may not always be the one standing under the lights. Instead, service is about lifelong learning, and taking the time to develop the right habits and spiritual disciplines required to strengthen your heart and mind. It should not happen with ulterior motives, but by using your gifts intentionally to help others. Most of all, service is about exercising your courage in the process of stepping up.

Simply put, stepping up is seeing an opportunity and doing something about it—noticing a need and filling that need. It's having the ability to stand in the gap so that the leader can better utilize his or her gifts of leadership. Whether an injustice or an instance of bullying, an inefficiency or a problem of productivity, an injury or an incident of interpersonal conflict, you can use your own abilities and influence in these opportunities to bring about change. As soon as you identify when and where to step up, you look to find solutions, to give encouragement, and to attempt to make that situation better—without worrying about what's in it for you. That's stepping up.

Many leaders throughout history have been able to become successful because those behind the scenes served with the end goal in mind. Those in supporting roles didn't need to shine themselves because contributing to the success of something larger was rewarding enough. Martin Luther King, Jr. stepped up when he saw injustice and inequality, but not without the likes of Bayard Rustin and Hosea Williams. Bill Gates stepped up when he identified inefficiency in technology, but not without Paul Allen or Richard Rashid knowing their role within the Microsoft dynasty. Mother Teresa stepped up to help the poorest of poor, the destitute, the sick, and the homeless, as countless others assisted on her journey to heal the world. Oprah Winfrey stepped up and forever changed the landscape of daytime television, but not without her best friend Gayle King supporting her and standing in the gap whenever needed. My friend Pastor Joel Osteen stepped up by taking a leadership role that he neither desired nor felt qualified to fill, and my purpose is to serve Pastor Osteen so that he can lead in the way that God has called him. Jesus Christ stepped up in the ultimate act of sacrifice by dying for all of us on Calvary so that we may live a life free from sin and full of His holy abundance—and even Jesus needed His disciples to help Him fulfill God's plan.

When each of these individuals started they were not known, but their ultimate calling was to LEAD. Yet they couldn't do that without those standing in the wings, willing to serve their cause.

Like many of us, you may not be called to lead but to SERVE. Not everyone chosen to serve will be called to lead, but it is a blessing to identify where you are called to be.

This process is not about religion, wealth, status, or fame. Your growth as a servant leader is about your humanity, your voice, and your willingness to be who you were made to be. When you finally engage with the present as an engineer of eternity, then it's a game-changer. Are you ready to quit settling for less than God's best in your life? Then it all starts now—by turning the page and *Stepping Up!*

CHAPTER ONE

The Inward Voice

"Everybody can be great, because everybody can serve."
—MARTIN LUTHER KING, JR.

Where you serve today can become where you lead tomorrow because you never know when God will promote you from a volunteer to a victor. I know firsthand what it means to serve because God has blessed me with increasing responsibility throughout my life. Through embracing that responsibility, often requiring that I put my own plans aside, God has fulfilled more through me than I could have imagined for myself. *Why me?* I wonder. I'm not the most talented or gifted, the best educated or spoken, the best looking (don't tell my wife!) or most successful. I'm just someone willing to serve faithfully where God wants me. And to my amazement, many times, God has wanted me to step up.

My parents set this example for my siblings and me as they raised us. My father in particular taught me about being faithful in doing the small things so that I would be prepared when larger opportunities came my way. I often saw this on the job with him, because immediately after finishing high school, I worked for his construction company in our hometown of Houston, Texas.

While I enjoyed working with my dad, I also began volunteering at Lakewood Church, where my family had been worshipping since I was nine. There, I helped with the church's growing television ministry. At first, I would do whatever needed to be done and ended up becoming a grip—someone who helps set up the camera—before stepping behind the lens to run the camera itself. I loved serving behind the scenes in this way, knowing that I was helping spread the Word to thousands, if not millions, of people watching our services being broadcast.

Little did I know that I would still be there thirty years later!

Stepping Out in Faith

Lakewood had just built a new 8,000-seat sanctuary. Due to this expansion, we moved the television ministry and equipment over to the new facility. Although I was still only a volunteer, I was learning so much. My dad always taught me that you can learn anything—all it takes is someone willing to teach you. If they're willing to teach you, you must be willing to learn. Even if you're not entirely sure why you're learning how to do something, when given the opportunity, learn all you can because you never know when it might be useful down the road.

Two men became great teachers for me during my time as a volunteer at Lakewood. The first was David Grundy, who really took me under his wing and mentored me. He taught me an array of skills such as film editing and how to use the special effects machine. Gary Meyers, our head engineer, was my other teacher. He kept our equipment running and taught me all kinds of ways to repair things when they went down. Because I was attuned to the knowledge these men shared with me in our day-to-day interactions, it prepared me for my time to step up—but I'd also need faith.

I remember a situation when one of our film editing machines broke down. I called Gary and described what had happened right before the problem occurred and what the stalled machine now looked like. This information helped him diagnose the issue, but because he was working offsite, he wouldn't be able to come fix it for several hours. So that meant we'd have to sit around for hours until he arrived to repair the machine so we could get our work done. We were on a tight deadline to finish the program, so there was no way I could waste so much time waiting for help when I had watched Gary make similar repairs numerous times. I decided to step out in faith, but I was already familiar with the path.

Unable to wait for Gary, I went to talk to Pastor Joel and said, "Hey, we can fix this. I've seen Gary do this before so I know which tools to use and how to make this repair. Do you mind if I try?"

"You sure?" he asked.

"Yeah, I got this—it's just common sense," I said. "Besides, I can't break it—it's already broken!"

Joel laughed with me and told me to go ahead. I unplugged the switcher, replaced the part, and in less than half an hour, the machine worked perfectly.

It wasn't long after that incident that Joel presented me with an opportunity. He and I had known each other since we were kids. We played baseball together, and growing up, we had been in and out of each other's houses. So I could tell he had something on his mind when he asked to see me before I left my volunteer shift that day.

"You do such a great job, Johnny," Joel said. "You have such a positive, can-do attitude all the time." He paused, aware of how uncomfortable yet appreciative I was of his compliments. "Would you be willing to move into a full-time staff position?"

"Thank you, Joel," I said, beaming. "I'm honored that you would ask me."

"I know you've been working for your daddy's construction company," Joel continued, "and I'm afraid this position would not pay as much. But I'd love to have you on board. Why don't you think about it, pray about it, and then if you're interested, we can discuss the details."

"Thanks, Joel," I said. "I'm definitely interested, but let me sleep on it."

I was about to step out in faith once again, only this path was not so familiar.

The Voice Within

✺ It's important to seek the voice of God through regular prayer and time with the Word. It's hard to describe—it might be more of a spiritual knowing than a sound—but the voice you hear within will help guide you to where God wants you to be.

Excited by the prospect of working for Lakewood Church and doing God's work—even if it was operating a camera and other broadcast equipment—after Joel made the offer, I prayed about it the rest of the day. But it was the following morning before I received an answer. When I woke up, Joel's offer immediately came to mind, and something within me, an inward voice, the whisper of God's Spirit, told me to accept the job.

Again, this wasn't an audible voice or my own voice in my head—just an awareness, a sense of God prompting me with His presence, a communication between me and the Holy Spirit. Looking back, it reminds me of the voice Samuel hears in the Old Testament. Serving as an apprentice to Eli, the boy Samuel was lying down when he heard someone call his name. He assumed it was Eli but the old man had not called him. After he heard the call three times, Samuel had been instructed by his mentor to respond, "Speak, Lord, for your servant is listening" (1 Sam. 3:9).

Samuel's experience tells us that we might not recognize God's voice at first. We may need to hear it repeatedly before we learn to discern the sound of His Spirit within us. And like Samuel, we always want to be receptive and obedient once we've heard God's message for us.

Confident of God's answer, I put in my notice and called Joel to accept his offer of a full-time position. My father accepted my notice, and although he was sad to see me go, he fully understood when I told him about hearing the inward voice. He knows that when the Lord speaks, you have to listen.

Although the work was different than construction, my father had always taught me to put my best foot forward. Dad had always told me that as long as I put in my best effort, I would succeed no matter what I was doing. He had also taught me not to compare myself to others and just to focus on being the best I could be. In my new role on the broadcast team, what I had already learned as a volunteer about filming, editing, and programming served me well. The rest I learned simply by doing, always eager to discover new dimensions to the work I was doing behind the scenes.

Listen with Your Heart

In my new role at Lakewood, God's voice continued to speak to me. Once we were having a staff meeting with Pastor John Osteen, Joel's father and our senior pastor, in attendance. Our meeting had finished, and everyone lingered to visit and catch up. Now, I have always paid attention to my surroundings and enjoyed observing people, and as I glanced at Pastor John, I sensed he needed something. Without speaking, I wondered to myself, *Now, what does he need?* and my inward voice answered immediately, "He needs some water."

So without questioning the rationale for this answer, I just slipped out and returned with a bottle of water, which I handed to Pastor John.

"How did you know I wanted water?" he said with a smile.

I felt embarrassed and unsure of how to explain. "Uh, I just thought you might be thirsty," I said.

"Hmm," Pastor John said with a gleam in his eye. "I better keep my eyes on you!"

We both laughed, went our separate ways, and I didn't think any more about it.

A few days later I was at work when my phone rang. I recognized his voice right away.

"Hey, Pastor John," I said. "How are you today?"

"I'm fine, Johnny," he said. "What are you doing right now?"

"Well," I said, looking at the machine on my desk, "I'm typing in Scripture on the character generator."

"Sounds good," he said. "Joel tells me all the time what a hard worker you are. We sure do appreciate how quickly you've jumped in and become such a big part of our ministry team."

"Thank you, Pastor John," I said. "That means a lot. I love being here!"

"Well, keep up the good work, Johnny. I'll talk to you later."

Grinning from ear to ear, I hung up the phone, grateful for

the way his encouragement had just made my day. But then that inward voice piped up.

"You missed something there, Johnny," said this voice.

What? I asked silently. *How did I blow it?* I immediately felt defensive and a little upset. It made no sense. I didn't lie or exaggerate in my conversation with Pastor John. What did I miss? I tried to get back to work but continued to feel confused and preoccupied by figuring out what was going on. One question echoed in my mind, "How did I blow it?"

That's when the inward voice answered, "The next time he calls, simply ask him what he needs. Let him know you're willing to help."

As I absorbed this response, I thought, *Are you kidding me? Of course, I'm willing to help, but I don't want to presume Pastor John needs my help for anything.* Still, I silently agreed that if and when he called again, I would respond accordingly. My peace was restored. I went back to work and didn't think about this internal conversation until two days later when Pastor John called me again.

"Hey, Johnny, what are you up to?" he asked after we had exchanged greetings.

The inward voice immediately prodded me with, "Remember what you should say?"

Without hesitation I said, "What are you in need of, Pastor John? How can I help?"

He proceeded to say he would like me to accompany him on an appointment. I not only went with John on that appointment, but I learned to display a willingness to serve every time he—or anyone else on our team—called. God's inward voice asked me to pay attention and hear the silent requests others were making. I learned to listen before I responded and leaped into action. I began to listen with my heart.

Follow the Peace

✺ If I hadn't learned to listen to my heart and obey that inward voice, I would have missed out on so much in life. I urge you to spend time in prayer so you can learn to discern when and how God speaks to you. Pay close attention to His voice. Sometimes what you hear might not make sense, but if you heed the voice and obey its instructions, you will experience peace. In fact, let peace be your umpire as you decide what's safe and what's out. We're told that God's peace surpasses all understanding (see Phil. 4:7), so let the peace you have overrule your doubt and insecurities.

If you focus on your fears, anxieties, and worries, then they will hold you back from God's best for your life. The enemy can't give you peace, only God can. The enemy will try to rob you of your peace by planting seeds of frustration, worry, fear, and doubt within you. But when you live by faith, then the inward voice will help guide you in choices that will make for a healthier and happier life. Remember, heeding God's voice will always be followed by inward peace.

I remember learning this shortly after becoming a pastor— yet another step of faith—when Paul Brady and I were invited to speak at a conference in Manchester, England. It was a great conference, and the people who attended were very blessed. Before we had finished, the organizers asked us to come back the following year to speak again, so naturally I was excited and honored that they wanted us to return. But as I was preparing for my final message there, the inward voice impressed upon me that it was time to go home and stay.

Now of course this was very confusing to me in that moment. New doors were being opened and new relationships formed, so why would I stay home next time when everything was going so well? Nonetheless, the message was strong and I had peace about accepting its truth. So, while giving my last sermon there, I shared what I had experienced in my room, especially after encouraging the attendees throughout the week to listen to God's inward voice and follow the peace.

In order to obey God's voice, I told the conference leaders that even though I had verbally committed to come back I could not do so. They of course understood, even though I still couldn't grasp why God would not want me to take this opportunity, through which I would be recognized and able to minister to thousands of people.

When I returned home, however, and pondered it some more, I realized God was giving me a choice. He said, "Would you like to minister to 20,000 people at one time, or would you like to support someone ministering to millions for a lifetime?" As soon as God put it like that, I knew it was a no-brainer! I knew my gifts and believed my calling to be in supporting

Pastor Joel, who had just accepted the call to replace his dad shortly after the Lord took Pastor John home to heaven.

At that time, I didn't know the church would grow by tens of thousands, that Joel's books would sell millions of copies, and that we would move yet again into a former sports arena. But when God revealed my path to me, I was overwhelmed with emotion and such a longing to return and assume my position. I surrendered my will to His perfect plan for my life, knowing that it was foolish to resist the divine destiny God had for me.

When God speaks, you learn to follow the peace.

Trust and Obey

When I've heard the inward voice, God has never asked me to come and debate with Him about whether or not it's what I should do—because He knows what tomorrow holds. He knows what the next minute holds. So why would I debate with somebody who knows everything? So I've learned to reason in my heart that what His voice tells me is right. I don't even have to understand it or find it logical. I simply need to trust Him and obey His instruction. It's our decision to follow God's direction.

When you follow the inward voice, it will lead you down the right path every time. Heeding the inward voice will set you up for blessings that keep coming and coming, season after season—far beyond what you can imagine or create for yourself. I remember that after I accepted Joel's offer to join the television ministry full time, I still second-guessed myself every now and then, wondering, *Did I make the right choice?*

But if you follow the peace, God never leads you down the wrong road. At the time I felt like I was making a big sacrifice to leave a good-paying job with my father's booming construction business. When I did my taxes at the end of that year, though, I realized I made more money than I would have if I'd stayed with my father. I was blown away! I marveled at the way God had blessed me. While I thought I was giving something up, He just wanted to bless me more.

God will never ask you to sacrifice something without blessing you in some way for your obedience.

In fact, the Bible says, "Obedience is better than sacrifice" (1 Sam. 15:22). And I don't think it's a coincidence that this truth comes from our old friend, Samuel, who learned firsthand about listening to God and obeying Him. I'm convinced that God prefers our obedience over anything else we can offer Him. When you are obedient, there is no need for a sacrifice. If you do what God says, you will never need to sacrifice.

If Adam and Eve had done what God told them to do and obeyed His instruction, there would never have been a need for a sacrifice. I think we would have still been in the Garden of Eden. But because of their disobedience, and the sinful nature we inherited ever after, we have to offer sacrifice to atone for our sins and to approach God. You see, relationships always cost you something, and a relationship with the Holy God of the universe should have the highest price of all. And please don't misunderstand—I'm not talking about blind obedience or following Him in some detached, closed-hearted kind of way. I'm talking about whole hearted obedience because you know His character and trust Him regardless of whether you understand.

You see, my friend, we always have choices. And perhaps the most important decisions we ever make are whether to obey God's voice in our lives. While it was my father's choice for us to join the fellowship at Lakewood Church, my choice came when I accepted Jesus into my heart and began my personal relationship with Him. From there, I had to decide to listen for God's voice and to obey Him when I heard it. This led to accepting the invitation to work for the church.

When you serve, it is a step toward your God-given destiny. Accepting that invitation to work for the church put me closer to Pastor John Osteen, which put me in place to become a blessing to him. I chose to sow seeds of service by working diligently and faithfully in the television ministry. Joel and others saw my natural ability to get things done. That step led me to a more elevated position in the church, where I could help one of the greatest pastors of all time. What a precious gift from God that Pastor John Osteen mentored me, blessed me, and spoke in my life.

Sowing Seeds of Service

❈ Most of the time, we can't see the big picture the way God can. We only glimpse a small piece. Paul said, "For now we see through a glass, darkly; but then face to face: now I know in part; but then shall I know even as also I am known" (1 Cor. 13:12 KJV). Even though we can only see a small piece through the "glass, darkly," if we just trust God in the midst of each choice and move forward, then we can be confident of the outcome. Now looking back, I'm so glad that I made the choices I made to obey God—and to receive His many blessings in the process. Throughout the domino effect of one decision toppling into the next opportunity for service, I've seen God's hand at work. I'm where I am now because of my love for helping the church.

Because when I started out I was just volunteering, I wasn't getting paid. I wasn't doing it for money but because of my love for God and my willingness to go where He wanted me to go. I wanted to help my church spread the Gospel so I offered to help. I began running the camera and doing whatever needed doing. Everything was based on helping someone.

So if you want to step up, let God take care of your promotion as you focus on serving his purpose with pure motives. You can't view roles of service as only stepping-stones for something greater. You can't give only to see what you can get. That's the essence of entitlement. You must give of yourself, open-handed and open-hearted, with no strings attached.

When I started to work with Joel back in the early days

of Lakewood's television ministry, I never considered where it would lead me. There was no grandstanding or showboating to see who would notice me and how I could climb the ladder and be a leader. The process simply started when I saw something that needed to be done and jumped in to do it. I couldn't wait on someone else to fix the editing machine because I knew God had equipped me with what I needed to repair it. *Why wait on someone else when I could just jump in and do it?*

I fear too many people serve only to be noticed. They're looking for those opportunities to show their gifts and talents in order to be recognized and valued and elevated to higher levels. But God tells us to keep our motives pure. He wants us to remain humble and willing to serve however He may ask us.

Everybody wants to take their shot—but why? What drives them—advancement for themselves or for God's glory? Many are looking for their ship to come in so they can experience their fifteen minutes of fame. But I suspect that if we chart history, the majority of people who have succeeded and achieved greatness did so by serving without any other motive than giving their gifts to the world's needs.

I never dreamed that my destiny would allow me to work, serve, and minister alongside a man who was my friend as a boy and now my pastor as an adult. A man who is not only my pastor but the leader of the largest church in our country. A man after God's own heart who reaches millions with the message of the Gospel. While I now serve under Joel Osteen,

I will always serve up. I will always serve God by listening to the inward voice of His Spirit and obeying Him each step of the way, one step at a time.

Throughout your life, no matter where you may be right now, you will continue to confront choices that lead you into your divine destiny. As you grow in relationship with God, His inward voice will speak to you. The choice is yours. Will you obey Him and experience joy and peace as you serve?

Your Next Step

At the end of each chapter, you will find a couple questions intended to help you personalize and practice the principles of stepping up covered in the chapter. These are designed to help you apply the material in my message and make it your own. You can simply think about your responses and reflect on your answers, but I encourage you to use a notebook or journal to write down your thoughts, answers, questions, and reflections in response to each chapter. As the Lord told the prophet Habakkuk, "Write down what I reveal to you so that he may run who reads it" (Hab. 2:2).

You will also find a short prayer provided to ignite your conversation with God in order to follow His guidance and direction. We all serve better when we serve the Lord! So, use these prayers to get started or your own words—but definitely seek God's power as you pursue the fulfillment of His promises in your life. Remember, you can do all things through Christ who strengthens you!

1. How have you seen God use past experiences in your life to equip you for your current leadership role? Could you see the value of these experiences at the time or only now in hindsight? What does this tell you about our limited view compared to God's limitless perspective?

2. When have you heard the inward voice of God speak to your heart? How has His voice placed a calling on your life to lead and to serve?

※

Dear God, thank You for loving me and saving me. Help me to hear Your voice as I seek to serve You in all that I do. Examine my heart, Lord, and remove any selfish motives that would prevent me from doing my very best for You and You alone. I want to hear the inward voice, trust Your truth, and step out in faith to obey You. I want to serve by listening, learning, and loving You more each day. Amen.

※

CHAPTER TWO

Staying in Your Lane

"The best way to find yourself is to lose yourself in the service of others."
—MOHANDAS GANDHI

Discovering what you do well and focusing on being the best you can be in that area is not always easy. The temptation to stray into other lanes instead of remaining on your own path arises regularly. But if you're going to step up, then it's vital to become an expert in your area of strength—not someone who's merely competent in various areas. Otherwise, you'll get stuck shifting from lane to lane but never gaining traction in any of them.

Growing up and helping my father on construction sites, I often witnessed this tendency in action. We built homes from the ground up. We did the ground plumbing, foundation, framing, electrical work, drywall, finish work, HVAC, and roofing—all of it.

When building a home, very few people can perform every

task. You need carpenters, plumbers, electricians, as well as skilled laborers and artisans, to work together to produce the final structure. A good contractor knows how to serve as a manager, like a conductor directing an orchestra, who brings each group in at the right time to do their job.

People in the homebuilding industry understand each other's craft but cannot do it all with a high level of skill. It takes years of practice to cultivate the expertise needed to master each aspect of construction and understand the different codes related to one's particular trade. Sometimes I witnessed a carpenter trying to wire a house or solve an electrical problem, but rarely did it work out. Knowing one's area of specialty does not mean you know someone else's, even if they're related in pursuit of a common goal.

Stepping up means putting in the time to master the Master's gifts in you.

Find Your Lane

Often we cross over into someone else's area, thinking we can do a better job even though we have not been properly trained. I've found this is often due to not discovering and embracing one's own gifts sufficiently. Without recognizing our God-given abilities and purpose, we often go through a process of trial and error. We have to discover the power of our unique gifts in order to lead effectively and step up.

It's so important to discover and unpack all God has placed inside you—both natural abilities and spiritual gifts—because no one can exercise them the way you can. This is because no one has the exact same combination of gifts as you. In the Bible, the Greek word typically used for talents and gifts is *charism*, which literally means favor or gratuity (see 1 Cor. 12:7, Eph. 4:10–12). Before we were even born, God graced us with His good gifts—all we would need and then some to fulfill the divine purpose for which He created us.

God has blessed each one of us with our special *charisms* as a source of power and purpose in our lives. He wants us to reflect His glory and goodness and show His love and goodness to everyone around us. We each have our unique function in the Body of Christ: "For just as each of us has one body with many members, and these members do not all have the same function, so in Christ we, though many, form one body, and each member belongs to all the others. We have different gifts, according to the grace given to each of us" (Rom. 12:4–6).

When you live out of your gifting, you feel alive and experience the joy and peace of the Lord. You're in your zone. You're in your lane and traveling at the right speed for all God calls you to do. You become the best version of yourself, realizing all that God created you to be, and your contribution makes this world a better place. You are salt and light, providing flavor and illumination to everyone around you.

Shifting Lanes

✺ Even once we know our gifting and begin traveling in our lane, we sometimes try to change lanes. We might grow tired or begin to burn out and wonder if we might be happier trying another area of leadership and service. If we're serving behind the scenes, we might crave the spotlight and want to be noticed and appreciated. Or maybe the grass just looks greener—or the pavement smoother, if I can mix my metaphors—when we see how others have been gifted and envy their success.

Drivers on the highway often see this same phenomenon. So often you see someone abruptly move into another lane without any signal or warning. Such reckless shifting sometimes causes an accident. If we must change lanes or feel called by God to try a new gift, then we need to communicate clearly. As we all learned in driver's ed, the best approach for changing lanes is to put on your turn signal to alert other drivers that you need to get over.

In the same manner, we should let someone know when we are entering their space. We should get permission first. I call it putting on your signal before changing lanes. Maybe you only need to pass through their territory briefly in order to complete another goal. Or you might be filling in for someone temporarily. Whatever the reason, the key is trying to let others know you're venturing into their lane.

Otherwise, you, along with the people upon whom you're encroaching, often suffer the consequences. Your car may not have been damaged in an illegal lane change, but it could easily damage other vehicles. When driving, we learn to diligently monitor our surroundings, aware of how we interact while observing the environment we're entering. As we quickly learn, we're not only driving to get somewhere, we're driving so that others may reach their destination safely as well. Stepping up always means thinking of how you can bless others.

If you're driving erratically, other drivers will honk at you to get your attention or to caution you to rethink what you were about to do. They may also flash their lights, wave you over, or brake to the shoulder. Similarly, we have to pay attention when others indicate they're coming into our lane. Always look for permission to proceed. It will keep you out of trouble.

We should always put ourselves in other people's shoes. If you feel that something would hurt you, it would probably hurt the other person, too. Jesus told us, "So whatever you wish that others would do to you, do also to them, for this is the Law and the Prophets" (Matt. 7:12). We know this as the Golden Rule, and it's golden because it reflects the timeless, loving mercy God shows to each of us as His children.

Let all be of one mindset, and ready to help each other. As individuals, we have to learn how to work as a team that will benefit each member by allowing him or her to do what he or she does best. When we pray for each other, it will help us keep our heart pure toward each other. When we pray for each other, it brings peace and builds unity. Praying for others will also remove strife and jealousy. It's tough to stay upset or angry with someone when you're praying for them. Praying for someone creates a strong bond between you and the person you pray for that cannot be easily broken.

Every decision has an effect on your tomorrow. We must recognize that the individuals who cross our path do not just do so by accident. They are in our lives because God has allowed us to meet for a reason.

Driving Lessons

✻ Being around greatness bestows great wisdom and knowledge that helps propel you into your destiny. It's like learning to drive from others who have been driving a long time. I had an opportunity to be around some great mentors in my life, and each one contributed to my ability to step up. My father and mother, of course, set the standard and demonstrated day in and day out what it looked like to follow Jesus and to serve others. My spiritual father, Pastor John Osteen, along with Doctor Freddie Frazier, Bishop Roy Lee Kossie, and many others, taught me that true leadership requires serving those around you.

Great mentors are a precious gift. You should not just let anyone speak into your life. Their words carry weight and can set you up for success or failure. Great mentors are transparent. They aren't ashamed about their mistakes or failures. Mentorship is really based on caring for another person and investing in that person's success. The best mentors love sharing their ups and downs because they know the importance of helping others.

You may say, "How do I recognize a mentor?" Easy—a mentor is someone you love being around. Every time you're in their presence, you're extremely inspired. Great mentors will always give you wisdom that transcends the moment and echoes into every area of your life. For example, my father taught me all he knew about building. When we would look at the plans for a new home, he would tell me to study the blueprint until I could look at the lot and see the finished structure as part of the landscape.

I have applied his wisdom about vision to so many areas of my life. The big lesson he taught me went beyond blueprints and construction. "Do not take the first step until you have the vision of success," he was saying. No matter what project, endeavor, or task I have tackled, I've always tried to envision the finished outcome. Basically, I try to look at the opportunity and see the result in its fullness before I even start. With an end-result vision in mind, you become better qualified and prepared for anything that comes your way.

Our dreams allow us to envision how we can lead and therefore also how we can serve. For example, Joseph was the greatest dreamer of all time. God gave him a dream that his entire family would serve him, which meant that he would eventually be a great leader. But along the way, Joseph frequently found himself serving others. At Potiphar's house, he was second in command. In the prison, he was in charge.

Finally, Pharaoh made Joseph second in command of all of Egypt because of his ability to interpret dreams and bring understanding to the dreams of people—a gift from God. God will always put anointing in us.

When you have an actual dream or passion for something, God will bless you with what it takes to step up and be a blessing to other people, to help them do what they need to do. So if you're in the ministry of trying to help someone, you must always realize that God gave you something, not just for yourself, but to be a blessing to everybody else. You can't keep it to yourself, you just can't hold it to yourself, and it can't just benefit you. It is meant to benefit other people too. And the more that you understand you're valuable and what you have to say is valuable, then you're going to be a blessing to people just by showing up.

Always Be Prepared

Even when we've discovered our gifts and are following our God-given dream, we must be active in preparing and exercising those gifts. It's like getting ready for a long car trip. You get your car's engine tuned up and fill up the gas tank. You don't wait until the last minute or assume you'll be able to wait until you're on the road. In other words, don't leave all the details up to God when He wants us to do our part to prepare.

Jesus told us that with people some things are possible,

but with God all things are possible (see Matt. 19:26). We must do our part—we focus on what's possible—and leave the impossible up to God. I think you have to put yourself in a position to do what you can. You have to take one step. When we take one step, God takes two.

A lot of people are waiting on God to do something, but really God says He's the author and finisher of our faith. He has already put in us what we need. Everything we need, God has already put in us from the foundation of the earth. So He's the author and finisher. Basically, we need to allow God to be God, and we have to unpack and use the gifting and anointing He has placed in us. We have to just carry it out, walk it out, and use what He gave us.

Preparation is simply getting ready for what He's calling us to do by using what He's given us. Preparation begins by recognizing what you've got to work with. I start the day off by saying, "God, you have already equipped me, but make me sensitive to the things that you want me to do today so at the end of today, Father, you will say, 'Well done, thy good and faithful servant.'"

Preparation is key to success. In order to be successful, you have to have a vision or plan before you. Preparation is laying out those plans, and I thank God that He says He's prepared. God uses the word *prepare* a lot, which is the root word of preparation. And so everything God does has already been thought out. Preparation means you've thought out and know what you're going to do, and you know the path you're going to walk on. It is basically like having a vision about something.

It's writing the vision and making it plain, so whoever reads it can run with it. It's not only for whoever reads it, but it's also for the writer. It keeps you on track—and it keeps you focused.

Focus on Now

❋ Focus is the key. When you're focused on something, you are propelled to it. I remember going on safari in Kenya when I went to Africa. We were traveling in a Hummer when we came upon a leopard standing as still as a statue. In fact, I thought it had to be fake, some kind of decoy or something because it wasn't moving even as we drove up alongside it. Then I saw the tail twitch ever so slightly. Still, that leopard did not even flinch even though we were within thirty yards of him. Why? Our guide told us that the big cat was focused only on his prey—something we couldn't even see from where we were.

We need that same kind of intensity and level of engagement as we pursue following our plan and bringing our vision to life. The Bible tells us, "Be harmless as a dove, but wise as a serpent" (Matt. 10:16). Like the leopard I saw in Kenya, a serpent knows how to maintain focus, remaining very still until it decides to strike. It remains undistracted by what's going on around it unless it's directly threatened.

Leaders who step up also know how to focus strategically. They keep their eyes on the prize. They don't let big things distract them. Staying focused means you don't pay attention to the distractions because distractions get you off point.

How do you stay focused? You have to meditate on your plan. The Bible says to meditate on His Word day and night (see Josh. 1:8). Why? So you can be successful by absorbing and following the guidelines God provides for us to live in accord with who He is and how He made us. If you want to be successful, then you learn to focus on the preparations God would have you make for moving forward. When you're prepared, then you can overcome. Basically, it's about setting goals. When you stay focused, you are remaining at the forefront of your mind. Anything that happens that is not a part of your goal is just a distraction.

Distractions can always get you off course. You have to ask yourself, *Is this going to help me, or will this detour me or get me off course?* You must simply do away with anything that gets you off course. No matter what the decision, you must focus on being prepared for what you're called to do. I think of how God told Abraham he was going to have a son. Abraham waited and waited and then couldn't imagine how such a thing was possible.

Often the full plan of what's in our hearts has not yet been revealed, but God has spoken, or someone has told us what's going to happen. So in your preparation, you have to remain patient.

Abraham wasn't patient, so he came up with another plan to bring about what God had prepared his heart for. Because he came up with his own plan, it caused problems. When you change lanes instead of staying in the lane you know God has anointed, you should expect some major detours.

I've experienced this concerning the schedule I keep as I serve Joel and our church. I've learned not to look ahead but just to live one day at a time. We have a very busy schedule, and if you ask me what we're going to be doing in two months, I won't be able to tell you. But I know what I'm responsible for doing tomorrow and have my eye on the next trip that's coming. That's how I stay focused. This way, I don't get overloaded with trying to prepare too far in advance and do too much ahead of where I am right now.

Otherwise, I begin to look at all the dates and become overwhelmed, and it affects my preparation. When I begin to think *I have to do this* and get so busy and consumed by the whole schedule, I can't really enjoy the moment. Looking too far into the future will pull us away from the things we need to do today and we won't be as successful. The job will not be done as best as it could when we put too much on our plates.

When you are prepared, you will be successful when the opportunity arrives. Part of being prepared is knowing your weaknesses and your strengths. If you know you're going on a trip, get ready and don't put yourself under the stress of unpreparedness. Even your body doesn't function as best as it can when you haven't prepared for what's coming; you remove all chance for enjoyment of what's to come.

Even with small matters—especially with details that you might be tempted to overlook—don't lose your focus and don't slack off in your preparation. Do what you know you need to do to get the job done. In my position working for Joel, my wife understands that at a certain point I begin to focus on preparations for my responsibilities. Knowing how much I love her, she appreciates that I am simply prioritizing what I need to do for my job.

For example, in assisting Joel, I know my phone has to be charged because he relies on me to keep track of his schedule. If he wants to know the time, he doesn't ask me but will often just pick up my phone and go by it. He knows the time on my phone is the same time as a satellite and will automatically adjust to the correct time zone when we're traveling. So even little things like charging my phone and making sure certain details are right matter.

When you're stepping up, you have to know the one you serve or are helping. You anticipate their needs and do all you can to make their job easier. You become part of solving any problem they face, removing any obstacle that pops up, or resolving any conflict that arises. They come to rely on you because they know you're prepared and focused.

The Time Is Right

❋ Finally, in order to stay in your lane and maximize your gifting, I encourage you to remain aware of God's timing—not your own or anyone else's—when stepping up and taking on more responsibility. The Bible says your gift will make room for you (see Prov. 18:16). So there will be a time when your leader or someone in authority over you will say, "It's time for you to step up. You have been trusted and proven yourself, so you can be trusted with even more." For example, if you serve in ministry, and if you know your leader is relying on God's timing and has no other agenda but to serve the Lord, then you can rely on their instruction. If, on the other hand, their motives are driven by their own plans or by their own ego or you feel that a boss's agenda for you doesn't align with God's, then stop in your tracks!

So many times, I've been approached by someone who has just heard me preach. Feeling blessed by the Lord's message and how His Spirit spoke to them through my humble words, these individuals try to offer me a compliment by saying, "Pastor Johnny, you sure can preach! It's time for you to start your own church!" I thank them and tell them how encouraged I am by their response, but I also let them know that I'm blessed to be ministering and serving where I am. It's not that I'm unwilling to start a church or new ministry, but I'm never going to even consider it without prompting from the Lord within me.

I remember one Sunday after I had preached, this one man was so adamant about my starting my own church and becoming a senior pastor. So after I thanked this man and he continued to go on and on about "Johnny's Church," I smiled and said, "Okay, if I'm going to start my own church, then here's what I need you to do. First of all, I need you to find me a church building. Second, I want you to find me a house to live in with my family. Then I want you to provide me a salary.

But most importantly, on Friday night or Saturday, I need you to come to my house and prepare a message for me."

This gentleman's eyes got big and he looked at me like I was crazy! I just continued smiling back at him.

"Pastor Johnny, what are you talking about?"

"When God tells me to go," I said, looking him in the eye, "that's what I am going to do. I will go where He directs me and do whatever He prompts me to do. Until then, I know I'm exactly where I need to be!"

When you have a dream and you have something in your heart that you want to do, be prepared and focused, but also expect to wait on God. His timing is perfect. Others may urge you to rush ahead and get in front of the Lord, but we all know getting ahead of God's timing never works out.

So when you're uncertain about the timing of taking a big step forward, find someone you can trust, someone who knows the Lord and also knows and cares about you. They will see a bigger picture than you're able to see at that time because your focus is on the dream at hand. Someone on the mountaintop can see the big picture while you're still climbing up from the valley. They can see so far ahead of you and provide you with a unique vantage point. So trust their judgment instead of those people who may mean well but basically just want you to jump ahead based on their human perspective, not God's eternal perspective.

When you seek the Lord's timing and get wise counsel, it will save you from destruction, heartache, and pain. I know many pastors and ministers who jump out there and start a church without conferring with their own pastor or spiritual leader. They may pray about it but don't listen or wait for God's answer. But then they go do their own thing and end up coming back disappointed and discouraged when their new ministry or church fails. But they can't blame God when they're not walking with Him and waiting on His timing.

Here's the thing about God: the minute you decide you want to do something, you cannot force it to happen. Only God controls and orders our days. He is the Lord of the harvest. The Bible tells us that to every purpose under heaven there is a season. God says in due season you will reap if you don't give up. He's the one that made the day. He orders the steps, not us.

You have to enter into and accept God's timetable. You will never get Him to run on your schedule. You must learn to stay in sequence with God's movements and not rush or delay because of your own preferences. He is leading the dance. You're in partnership with God. You're doing a waltz with God. He leads and you keep step with Him and no one else.

Or think of it this way. You have to recognize the season you are in and know how to dress for the season. If it's summertime, you have to recognize and dress according to the season—short sleeves, light fabrics, cool garments. In winter, you dress in layers of wool and woven fabrics to keep out the cold. Similarly, your attitude has to be in preparation to the season of your life. And your decision-making process has to be according to the season in your life.

No matter what the season or weather you may be facing,

trust God to see you through it. Even when you get tired of your lane or wander outside the lines, don't give up. Always remember that God has a great plan for your life. Stay focused and trust that He can redeem your routes even when you're lost and way off track. Do not allow your past failures or mistakes to make you think that you are not qualified. God chose you knowing the mistakes that you would make.

It's only when you get off course on life's journey and start going off on your own tangent that you need to worry about getting lost. When you're on track, you experience God's peace because you know you're obeying His voice and aligned with His purposes for your life. If you get off course a little, it is just a matter of repenting or asking for forgiveness, and after that, the rerouting will take place. Put all you've got—body, mind, heart, and soul—into serving where the Lord has led you. Stay focused, stay prepared, step up, and wait on His timing.

If you stay in your lane, then I guarantee God will take you to your divine destination!

Your Next Step

1. Have you embraced your gifts and the primary lane where God wants you to travel, or are you still discovering them? Where do you believe God wants you to focus your time, attention, and energy right now? Why?

2. When have you shifted into others' lanes, either intentionally or accidentally, and realized you were not where God wanted you to be? How did you correct your detour? What did you learn from this experience?

✻

Lord, You tell me that I am wonderfully and fearfully made. You promise me a plan and a hope for my future, and I know that You're leading me into the areas where I can step up as I serve you. Empower me to focus on the lane You have given me and not to be distracted or tempted by other lanes. Help me to prepare for where I'm going in order to fulfill the potential You've placed inside me. I give You thanks and praise and all the glory! Amen.

✻

CHAPTER THREE

Understanding Your Position

"The place God calls you to is the place where your deep gladness and the world's deep hunger meet."
—Frederick Buechner

U nderstanding your position liberates you to give yourself wholeheartedly in service to those around you. From my experience, identifying where you are and recognizing whether it's where God wants you to be are crucial keys to your success. Although no two people's positions are identical— even those in the same roles execute them differently—it's vital for you to assess how well you fit into the place where you currently serve. Generally, most people's positions fall into one of three categories: millstones, stepping-stones, or milestones.

When you struggle in your position, it's important to be able to distinguish between what I call millstones (positions dragging you under) and stepping-stones (roles that God often uses to bridge your progress from one position to another). Although both millstones and stepping-stones provide unique challenges and stretch you beyond your own abilities, it is stepping-stones that draw you closer to God and make you stronger. Millstones, however, do just the opposite. They can be deadly.

Further, when you're in the right position—what we'll explore momentarily as milestones—God's favor will be on your life. As you serve using the gifts with which He has blessed you, you experience contentment, and your satisfaction, in turn, creates a domino effect of blessings for others. Life tends to flow so much better when you're doing what you know you were made to do. Everyone cannot be the chief, but when you're in your right position, you're the chief of that territory. You were designed for that position and have been equipped and prepared to fulfill its responsibilities.

The Daily Grind

❈ Now I'll be surprised if you've ever heard of a millstone outside of the Bible. In ancient times, millstones were familiar to most people as being essential to the process of grinding grain into flour. The process actually involved two stones: one that served as a stationary base and another that would turn and grind against it to crush the grains. We can assume that the Jewish people considered millstones an important tool in daily life because in the Old Testament we're told, "Do not take a pair of millstones—not even the upper one—as security for a debt, because that would be taking a person's livelihood as security" (Deut. 24:6).

In order to work effectively, millstones were known to be large and heavy, and other biblical references reflect this as common knowledge. In the Book of Job, a beast known as Leviathan is described as having a chest as hard as a lower millstone (see Job 41:24). Gideon's son Abimelech died when someone dropped a millstone from a tower above him, crushing him (see Judg. 9:53).

Perhaps the best-known reference, however, occurs in a comment Jesus made: "If anyone causes one of these little ones—those who believe in me—to stumble, it would be better for them if a large millstone were hung around their neck and they were thrown into the sea" (Mk. 9:42). In other words, if you lead a child of God into sinning, then you bring a crushing judgment against yourself. It would be better to drown because a millstone pulled you under than to cause someone else to stumble.

Similarly, what I call millstone positions grind you down in ways that are clearly harmful and dangerous to your physical, emotional, and spiritual health. They crush you under the weight of overwhelming responsibilities and duties for which you are not equipped—perhaps for which no one is equipped! I'm not talking about the hard work we must invest in any position or the suffering experienced from sacrificing our own agenda in order to serve others. Millstone positions are dead ends that trap you, often in ways you can't see because you're so frantic in trying to fulfill them.

How do you recognize a millstone position? It's certainly not just about the way you feel in your position, although your emotions and attitudes over time usually reveal the kind of position you're in. Millstones produce disappointment, discouragement, and depression and tend to send you spiraling down with little hope of escape or growth. You feel stuck in these roles, taken for granted by your supervisor and colleagues, overlooked for promotion, and sidelined from using your greatest gifts.

Once you recognize yourself in a millstone position, you must seek God's guidance for how to get out from under its weight. Draw on His power and seek the new path He has for you. After they escaped slavery in Egypt, the people of Israel wandered in the desert for forty years before entering the Promised Land. Their wandering was the result of their own disobedience, discontent, and distance between them and God. But the Lord is faithful and always provides an exit strategy for those who love and serve Him. Just as He parted the Red Sea for the Israelites to escape Pharaoh's army, God will open a way through your millstone position.

Take the Next Step

✺ We often linger in millstone positions longer than necessary because we chose to be there and put ourselves in that role. Maybe the job looked good when you were hired or a key relationship seemed dynamic at first, but you quickly felt its weight come crashing down. Your insecurity can be an open door to a bad decision or a regrettable mistake. When you desire a role or position that was not meant for you, you discover that you're unprepared for even basic aspects of its execution. Every challenge will be so much harder because you're out of position.

It's like what would happen if the quarterback changed positions with the center on the football field. The quarterback typically doesn't have the size to keep the defensive lineman out. The center doesn't have the agility to move and avoid being sacked as he finds a target to receive a pass. The only way to achieve victory is to be the best at your position—not anyone else's. Your success contributes to your team's success.

Serving is an honor—not a punishment or dishonor. If you want to lead and step up, then you must be aware that everyone serves someone else. No matter how high on any ladder you climb, someone is above you and someone is below you. Jesus Christ, the greatest and most secure person to ever walk the face of the earth, made this profound statement, "I didn't come to be served, but to serve" (Matt. 20:28). If anyone deserved to be elevated above every human being, surely it was our Savior. But rather than waiting for others to treat Him like the king He is, Jesus mingled among the masses and messes of life. He hung out with fishermen and tax collectors, prostitutes and lepers. He healed the lame and fed the five thousand. Christ's example inspires us all to be the best servant we can be wherever we may find ourselves.

We think being close to our leaders will give us the greatest insight on what makes them tick so that we can duplicate their success. While we can certainly learn from them, if we want to be the best we can be, then we must look beyond them to the Author and Finisher of our faith. The Originator of our lives knows all there is to know. The Bible tells us to acknowledge Him in all our ways and He shall direct our path (see Prov. 3:6).

Seeking God's guidance and direction—and not just following in your boss's footsteps or anyone else's—ensures you will proceed to your divine destination. So even if you sometimes struggle in your position, you know that you're on your way to your divine destiny. I call such positions stepping-stones.

Stepping Out in Faith

Stepping-stones provide some measure of fulfillment as you utilize your gifts and abilities. These positions are also usually challenging, but their challenges produce growth instead of stagnation. Your hard work gets recognized and appreciated. You gain valuable experience and expertise through the process of serving in stepping-stone positions. In these bridge positions, you also learn to rely on God on a daily basis. You realize that He has anointed you to serve in this place and will use it for your good and the good of His kingdom.

In stepping-stone positions, you develop close relationships with your supervisor, boss, or leader. Trust grows between you as you serve together and reach shared goals. You appreciate this person and respect them, and your dedication shows in the ways you serve. Such service includes being attuned spiritually to their needs, which includes praying for them daily.

Of course you support your leader from a physical standpoint, but again, the greatest way you can support your leader is through prayer. Pray for your leader by saying, "God, give them what they need. Thank you for their anointing." And have a heart of thanksgiving toward your leader and support your leader in prayer and fasting and whatever God puts on your heart for you to do. When you pray for your leader, I believe it's a covenant connection to God, that He will deposit in you what your leader needs and what your role is to your leader.

When you pray for the one you serve, you will begin to recognize change before everyone else. Do not let your position become common to you. When you begin to take your position for granted, you begin to take the individual for granted. Becoming too familiar with a person can also be dangerous. I have learned how to recognize and sense the moment. I always follow the lead of Pastor Joel. Like one learns in any profession, you know when it's serious work time or time to relax. By following his lead, I develop a complementary rhythm that facilitates and enhances my ability to serve him.

People often ask me how I've handled conflicts or disagreements with my boss, but our personalities are so similar that we have honestly never faced that kind of friction. Neither of us is perfect, but we understand each other and know how to communicate effectively. I realize our relationship is unique, and due in part not just to our similar temperaments but also to the trust and history of a forty-year friendship. While you likely will not have this kind of long-term relationship, you can nevertheless seek to build one by focusing on how best to serve those supervising you.

You got invited into the position because of serving. If serving got you invited, then serving will keep you in the room. Opportunities to step up always come about through serving. When you have been given the privilege to serve someone, never take it for granted. It never makes you better or more special than anyone else. When you take on that posture, it will only inflate and feed your ego. Serving is definitely a place of honor based on humility and loyalty.

When you serve someone, you will get to see them lead in a variety of settings. I am so blessed because Joel is the same in public and in private. What you see is what you get! No matter what he's doing or where he is, my boss is a genuine, humble, kind man seeking to follow Jesus' example. I know many people, however, who struggle with how to reconcile the public image of their leader with the private individual they glimpse in other settings. My counsel is simply to remember that while their boss may be anointed for their role, they are also human. Jesus is the only perfect person who walked this earth so we must focus on serving our leaders with compassion, consideration, and concentration on the positive.

In most working relationships, your loyalty will eventually

be tested. You will have to decide whether you want to serve with honor or serve with ambition. Serving with honor requires refraining from judgment whereas allowing ambition to drive you might lead to gossip, manipulation, and disloyalty. When your supervisor makes a mistake or disappoints you, focus on how Jesus would handle the situation. Our Lord taught us to live by the rule of treating others how we'd like to be treated. It is not our job to be the judge, jury, and reporter for someone else's mishaps. We must take care of the log in our own eye before we point out the speck in someone else's (see Matt. 7:5).

What Happens in the Tent

✳ Taking care of the log in our own eye forces us to look at our own sin before focusing on the flaws of others. Sin means you have missed the mark of what God has in store for you. When you try to capitalize or advance yourself by exploiting the sins of others, you choose to live beneath your privilege. In those opportunities when others fail, you have the opportunity to demonstrate grace, forgiveness, and generosity of spirit.

We have all heard the story about Noah building an ark and living on it for forty days and nights. That alone is a great feat. But one day, Noah got drunk and was naked and lying in his tent. (A little side note: If I'd been in his shoes, I would have probably taken a drink and gotten naked as well—after spending forty days on the ark with family and those animals!)

The story goes on to say that when one of Noah's sons, Ham, saw his dad's condition, he went out and talked about it. The other sons, Shem and Japheth, walked in backward so as not to look at their father's nakedness, and they covered him. When Noah woke up, he found out what had happened and cursed Ham and blessed the other sons. Why? Because basically whatever happens in the tent stays in the tent!

Even in our own lives, we have to operate with discretion because everyone handles tension differently. They may not be mature enough to handle whatever may occur. Never do things to make someone look bad and never reveal another's mistake to your boss so that you can look good in their eyes. Always go to the person who messed up first, because they might not have recognized their mistake. We are a team working together for one purpose—to facilitate and bring the vision to pass.

That type of behavior (making someone look bad or revealing another's mistake) will only bring division. The Word says that where the brothers dwell together in unity, there God commands the blessings (Ps. 133:1). To "dwell" means to live there or simply stay in that frame of mind. When you dwell there with your brothers and sisters, in peace and understanding, the blessings will continually flow on everyone involved. When you think of your boss as being a pen and your coworkers as fingers, only two fingers actually touch the pen: the thumb and index finger. However, the three other fingers, although they might not ever touch the pen, bring balance and help with the motion of the hand when writing.

If you're in a stepping-stone position, remain secure in that role. Don't rush to move on too quickly or jump ahead of God's timing. Give yourself completely and fully to doing your best as if unto the Lord. If you're a pinky, be the best pinky that you can be. You were designed for that which no other finger can do. If another finger tried to take over your role, it would be out of place. The thumb would look very funny where a pinky should be!

Never value what you do in your position based on who sees it or knows about it. God Himself has ordained, called, and chosen you to be a pinky before the foundation of the earth. God never makes a mistake, so never think that you are a mistake. What He has called you for is who you need to become. Never say you do not have what it takes. You were born with everything you need to fulfill your destiny; you just have to develop it and cultivate it.

Reaching a Milestone

Milestone positions are those places where you know you're in your element and firing on all cylinders. You know you're exactly where God wants you and can see how so many of your past experiences—mistakes and failures included— have prepared you to lead and serve in this place. Milestones may feel like reaching a summit—a new place requiring more responsibilities even while providing more rewards. Over time, milestones may give way as God leads you to follow Him to another summit.

Simply put, the key to reaching a milestone position is to always focus on serving.

A lot of people want to be served. But in order to be served, and more importantly to lead, you must first serve. Remember, again, Jesus said, "I didn't come to be served, but I came to serve." Basically by offering himself up as a sacrifice to serve mankind, now we serve him. This is how we follow his example. You may eventually lead and have others serve you, but that's not your objective. Don't go in trying to be served and you don't manipulate the situation. Don't force yourself into what you think is your milestone position because as Scripture says, "Your gift will make room for you" (Prov. 18:16).

A lot of people are trying to make room for themselves. They try to race up the ladder of success to achieve one milestone after another without considering where God wants them. When *you* make room, it means you're trying to do something based on your own ability and what *you* want, rather than following God's lead and submitting to His authority over your life. Even if it's regarding a position in the church, you must not assume that you know how best to serve. For instance, say you're a supervisor serving under the manager. You might have more natural leadership ability than he or she does, but if you think you're entitled to his or her position because your ability is better or stronger or because you're more gifted or more attractive, or whatever, then you've failed before you've even started.

A servant heart is the key.

Success in milestone positions requires servanthood.

Move to the Rhythm

❋ The key to best serving others with your leadership is by letting the Spirit of God lead you. You have to be led by the Spirit of God because otherwise you will get drained, you will get burned, and you will get worn out. There are so many pastors, leaders, and people in all sorts of leadership roles who are just worn out. Why? Because they're trying to help everybody and their resources are being depleted. Their anointing is being depleted. Why? Because they are moving out of sequence with God.

God is a God of rhythm. He has a beat. And His rhythm is about us being in sequence with Him to help somebody. And even though in our heart of hearts we want to help somebody, everybody that we come into contact with is not ready to be helped. Even though they might say they are, God knows their heart. Scripture tells us that we look at outward appearances, but the Lord knows what's inside the heart (see 1 Sam. 16:7).

Only God can look at the heart of a person. We can try to see the true character of a person, but no matter what we see, we must avoid having a judgmental spirit toward others. We have to see people through the mind of Christ, and through the eyes of the Spirit, and through the character of God as we look on them.

Basically we're asking, "God what will you have me do?" God is a perfect gentleman and models accordingly what we should do. And being a perfect gentlemen, in the Bible, He says, "Acknowledge me in all your ways and I will direct your path" (Prov. 3:6). So in any situation, God sits back on the sidelines until we ask him, "God, what will you have me do?" Then, we invite Him into the game. Once we invite Him into the game, we're sure to win because He never loses. But the thing is, for us to have success in life, we have to say, "God, come be a part of this. Teach me. Show me."

Once God has shown us something, then we must practice it regularly. We must use our gifting to anticipate the needs of those we serve. I love it when Joel asks me to handle a situation, complete a task, or resolve a problem, and I can say, "You're living in the past!" He knows by now what I mean by this: "It's already taken care of! I've already done it, so now you can focus on the present and future."

Often these are little details, but they have serious consequences if left undone or if they're completed poorly. The Bible says, "The little foxes spoil the vines" (Song of Sol. 2:15). I've also heard it said as God being in the details. And I know it's true because I believe it's the little things that bring life to the vine.

For example, let me share a story about a recent incident. At our church, we have a Planning Center Online (PCO) app on our phone. Without really knowing why, I was preparing for a service and felt it impressed upon me that I should open that app on my phone. It seemed logical because the app includes the order of service, specific Scripture used, worship songs, and so on. It just seemed like a good idea to have this information handy, and I felt prompted by the Holy Spirit to make sure it was readily available.

Sure enough, about two minutes later, Joel asked me, "What song is my cue to head to the pulpit?" I smiled, and without delay, I told him and showed it to him on the app.

"Wow, thank you, Johnny!" he said.

This moment is definitely an example of one of those small details that may seem inconsequential. If I had not had the app at hand, would it have destroyed the service? Would it have caused Joel to delay? No, but it would have hindered the flow of our service and could have thrown him off sync. It may seem like common sense, but you would be surprised how many times we can easily let details slip through the cracks. If we want to achieve and lead in milestone positions, we must be willing to follow God's prompting, trusting that He's preparing us for what will be needed later.

Power of Persevering

※ Understanding your position will require you to discern the kind of demands of the position you're in. Millstones, stepping-stones, or milestones—all three include unique struggles, but you want to be sure you're following God's lead and investing the gifts He has given you. Regardless of which position you're in, stepping up in faith may require you to go against what others say or want you to do.

I recall that back in 1974, when my family began to attend Lakewood Church, we caught grief from friends and family for attending a church that was largely white at the time. Then more than now, Sunday morning was the most segregated time during the week. Most people went to churches composed of people of their own race and ethnicity. When we started going to Lakewood, my parents were ridiculed by others, who said, "Why are you going to that white church with a white pastor?"

But my dad knew he felt led by God to go there. As the leader of our family, along with my mother, he made that choice. And if he hadn't made that choice and if he had buckled under pressure, then all of us would have missed out on so many incredible blessings over the years. But he stood his ground and followed through on what he knew the Lord wanted him to do. And there's power in persevering. Today, I enjoy the benefits of my father's obedience by serving in this major milestone position at which I've been called to serve.

Often when you make God-driven choices, you have to trust the Lord and stand behind your choice. Even though you might not see the big picture of your choice, you trust that God always knows what He's doing and has you where you are for a reason. You must look beyond outside influence and remain faithful as you follow a path others may not understand. The Bible says, "The steps of a righteous man are ordered of the

Lord" (Ps. 37:23). When God orders your steps, sometimes it may seem difficult to keep walking, but it's because opposition will come against us. We must realize that no matter what it is, we have to stay true to the choice that we've made and allow God to lead, because in the whole big scheme of things we'll end up saying, "Look where I am today."

You shouldn't buckle when someone says, "You know what, that's not for you. I can't see you doing that." That's their perception. But what is God's perception? What is God saying? What did God tell you to do? Always, at the end of the day, obey God. God is the one who has called you. God is the one who has anointed you. And God is the one who appointed you.

So no one else can disqualify you. You only disqualify yourself. And how do you disqualify yourself? By disobeying God. God never set you up for failure. He set you up to bless you. So just trust God in those moments when you say to yourself, "You know what, I know I heard from God. I'm going to stay true to the course." This way, it's not just hearing, "Well done, thou good and faithful servant" when you get to heaven. It's knowing, "Well done, thou good and faithful servant" at the end of every day. That's what we should strive to hear as we ultimately serve the Lord—no matter what position we're in.

When you strive to serve Him first, then your life is more fulfilled, not because you do everything perfectly each day, but because you're doing your best unto the Lord, and that's all He asks. God sees the heart and rewards us accordingly. Ultimately, understanding your position reflects your willingness to rely on God.

Your Next Step

1. How would you describe your understanding of your current position of servant leadership? Do you believe your current position is more of a millstone, stepping-stone, or milestone? Why? What next step do you need to take in order to lead and serve more effectively?

2. When have you been able to step up and serve others more effectively by following God's guidance? What role does your faith play in how you lead and serve? How often do you rely on God to direct your steps?

Heavenly Father, I thank You for leading me to my current position. As I look back, I can see how Your hand has faithfully guided me, prepared me, and equipped me to be in this role and serve those You have called me to serve. Help me to rely on You and the guidance of Your Holy Spirit in my daily actions and choices, so that I may remain attuned to all the ways I can serve those around me. Give me Your strength and power and let the humility of Jesus be my example in all that I do. Amen.

CHAPTER FOUR

Chosen by the Father

"Struggle is a never ending process. Freedom is never really won—you earn it and win it in every generation."
—CORETTA SCOTT KING

M any people work hard to step *up* when really they need to step *down*.

Let me explain what I mean by this. Often I see so many people who strive and chafe at their current position because they consider it merely a stepping-stone. They believe if they work hard enough that they can reach their next milestone sooner and advance quicker. They rely on their own power because they're impatient.

Even when they know they're answering God's call and trying to be obedient, they still try to outrun the Lord's timing. They assume that in order to step up and be the leader God calls them to be, they must do it based on human standards of advancement. They have fallen into the trap of our culture that conditions us to believe that only the men and women at the top of their company's organizational chart matter.

The reality is that we are not all called to be leaders as the world defines it. We may not be recognized by our human resources department, the board of directors, the deacons, the ladies' auxiliary, the PTA, our coaches, our teachers, our bosses, the campaign committee, or the awards presenters. We may not attain the promotion or win popular approval.

We must step down from the ladder we're climbing or the mountain we're scaling and follow God's path. Jesus said, "For whoever wants to save their life will lose it, but whoever loses their life for me will find it" (Matt. 16:25). Sometimes if we truly want to step up and move in God's direction, then we must step away from our own.

Behind the Scenes

※ God has chosen you to serve, to lead, and to step up—no matter where you are right now. In fact, He has brought you to this place and time in your life in order for you to grow into your next role, no matter what that may be, regardless of your title or how others see you. Ultimately, He may be leading you to a role of servant leadership, supporting another leader, another relationship, another business, another ministry, or another cause distinct from your aspirations. We should aspire to serve the Lord our God with all our heart, soul, and mind. Therefore, wherever He leads us, we follow and serve Him with gladness.

So many times, we think we want to be the one in the spotlight, at the head of the boardroom, in the corner office, in the pulpit, on stage, in front of the camera, or in the top position in our field—whatever that may be. But deep down, we know that is not really what we want or what we're made for. So many people remain discontent in their positions because they think they want to be higher up on the ladder when, in fact, they do not have the gifting, temperament, or desire to serve in those more public, front-and-center, solo kinds of roles.

We have been conditioned by our celebrity culture, by other people, by social media, by our Twitter-follower, me-first world to believe we only matter if we're on top. That we're only worthy or valuable if we are the star of our own show, both literally and figuratively. But this is not what stepping up is all about. This is not what answering God's call and serving diligently are all about. Those roles lead up—vertically and directly to God Himself. We don't have to climb any ladder to enjoy a relationship with the Almighty.

So we must recognize that our leadership positions, job titles, and ministry roles do not necessarily include a progressive ascent in this life. Not everyone gets promoted every two years and groomed to take over. Not everyone needs to be senior partner or CEO or sit at the top. As we see in the Bible, it's often the people serving the ones in authority who wield even more leverage to accomplish God's purposes.

Fearless in Faith

✺ Just consider Daniel, for instance. His willingness to serve, while in exile no less, became a turning point for the Jewish people. After King Solomon's rule over Israel, the nation unraveled. It didn't take long, just a few generations, for the ten northern tribes of Israel to abandon their faith in God and worship idols instead. The Lord sent warning after warning through His prophets, only to be ignored by His people, so He allowed the Assyrians to conquer the northern kingdom of Israel (see 2 Kings 17:16–23).

Israel's southern kingdom, composed of Judah and the smaller tribe of Benjamin, didn't fare much better. Even after seeing what happened to their northern kinsmen, they, too, ignored the messages of God's prophets Jeremiah, Habakkuk, and Zephaniah. So the Babylonians, led by Nebuchadnezzar, captured Judah and destroyed Jerusalem. The Israelites were captured as prisoners of war and taken back to Babylon to become slaves. As one of these exiles, Daniel faced a bleak future with no hope of rescue or restoration. His country was in ruins, the temple had been looted, and his people were slaves.

Nevertheless, Daniel refused to abandon his faith in God. Daniel continued to pray, to trust, and to reflect his relationship with the Lord in how he carried himself. Daniel balanced personal humility with confidence in God, and his captors noticed this difference. Daniel's strength of character displayed respect for these hostile pagan people who did not serve his God, and yet this young man refused to bow to Babylonian customs and culture, including commands from the emperor himself. Consequently, Daniel influenced those around him in a way no one else could have. Although he probably could not see it at the time, he was exactly where God needed him to serve.

For seven decades of his life—*seventy years*, just think about that—Daniel endured tests, challenges, and life-threatening danger. He watched his friends Shadrach, Meshach, and Abednego forced into the fiery furnace and yet emerge not only alive but without a single burn or singe. Daniel faced down the hungry beasts in the lions' den, trusting God to see him through. Time and time again, he obeyed God despite what may have seemed safe, logical, or in his own best interest.

No matter what he faced, Daniel's face never wavered. He was fearless in his faith. Consequently, Daniel garnered the respect and admiration of four different Babylonian leaders until Cyrus freed the Jewish people and allowed them to return to Israel. Daniel was never king, emperor, or a well-known prophet in his day, but the Lord used his faithfulness to save the Jewish people. Now that's stepping up!

The Choice Is Yours

It's hard to imagine remaining faithful in light of all the trials Daniel endured. He could easily have played the victim card and blamed God, the Babylonians, or other people. Daniel could have balked and withdrawn from God and let himself sink into depression and despair. Or he could have tried to be the hero and organize an escape from his captors. But instead, Daniel remained faithful, knowing that God was still with him even in that hostile land, even in dangerous situations, even in unbearable conditions.

If we want to step up and grow as leaders, then we, too, must refuse to be victims of our past or slaves to our circumstances. We must let God meet our needs and guide our steps. Serving Him must become our motivation and the source of our identity.

Sometimes I suspect we are trying to win the approval of others to compensate for the love, acceptance, and affirmation we did not have but desperately needed as children. Every child craves the approval of their father and mother, and many experience the unconditional love that two healthy, stable, devoted parents can bring. Others of us, however, did not get the nurturing love and affirming attention we needed in order to feel confident of our character and abilities. So we seek it elsewhere—often by working for it.

Some people find solace in relationships, both healthy and dysfunctional, while others try to escape their pain by going down destructive paths of addiction. Still others seek socially acceptable ways of getting the love, attention, and approval of those around them by becoming workaholics or by climbing the career ladder as fast as possible regardless of the cost to their families and coworkers.

Parents have the power to set the course that will affect the lives of their children. They have the power to bless their children and to point them toward their futures. Parents also have the sacred responsibility to teach their sons and daughters about the Lord. The Bible tells us, "Train up a child in the way he should go, and when he is old he will not depart from it" (Prov. 22:6, NKJV).

Fathers, in particular—in my experience—have a powerful responsibility resting upon their shoulders and the choices they make. My father made a decision that has been such a great blessing on my life. His choice launched and placed me in the position I am in today. It has been said, "Your character is the sum total of your habits and your habits are the sum total of your choices." My father had the ability to bless his children with his choices and he did.

We all have this same opportunity. Your choices are yours to make. Your decisions are controlled by and affect your free will. Every day you'll have choices before you, and when you make the right ones, I promise you will be smiling at night. The quality of your life is based on the quality of your choices. Your choices are influenced by your thoughts. Think on what is right, good, and holy, and then you will act accordingly.

Generational choices are so important to bless our success. The choices that my father made absolutely affected my destiny and some of the things that have happened in my life. But generational choices do not determine who you are and where you're going. We live in a world, even in the church, where people often talk about generational curses. But your future depends not so much on any generational curse; your future depends on your generational *choice*.

You have the choice to break the sins of your fathers and mothers and any consequences that you have suffered as a result. You have the choice to know and embrace your full identity in Christ as a child of God created in His image. You have the choice to follow God into a liberating, joyful, purpose-driven future.

While it may be tempting to think the bad thing that happened to Dad and to Grandpa is going to happen again, the truth is that you have a choice. No matter how bleak, how painful, how abusive, how impoverished, or how terrible your upbringing may have been, you still have a choice. You have the choice to realize that you have been chosen by your Heavenly Father for greater things.

I am so blessed because my parents not only loved me but also chose to raise me in a loving church community. I would say that the choice of my parents was so crucial to not only my life but also their lives and those of my siblings as well. But if they didn't make that choice, I wouldn't be where I am today. Not that God could not have brought me to where I am by some other route, but He blessed me with Godly parents who set me on a path for serving in my current role.

Even though my parents blessed me with their choices, I still had to choose whether I would serve the Lord and obey His call on my life. You have the same opportunity to decide your direction. God never forces Himself or His guidance on us. He loves us too much.

Power in Peace

※ If we read the Bible, we learn that God always gives His people a choice. For instance, consider the way He gave Abraham, then known as Abram, a choice: "The LORD had said to Abram, 'Go from your country, your people and your father's household to the land I will show you'" (Gen. 12:2). God told Abram to make a choice. The Lord said if you follow Me, then leave your hometown and say goodbye to your kinfolk, and I will show you a place to go.

Notice God did not say specifically the name of this place, or how long it would take to get there, or what it would look like exactly. When making choices, often you can't see the benefit of the choice you're going to make. You just stand at the crossroads and see the opportunity. You just have to trust God. Making the choice to step up and follow God comes from something deep within you. *"You know what, I'm going to make this choice. I feel peace. I know it's where God wants me. So I will let go of the path I was following and follow the Lord."*

Keep in mind that this kind of obedience may not make sense at the time. Don't expect others, even close family and friends, to always understand. Such choices cannot be determined by money or what will look good on your resumé. You make choices by being led by what you believe is right, not only according to God's Word but also by the conviction instilled in you through the Holy Spirit.

When you make the right choices, the reward will come eventually, but your choice must be based on peace—not what you see, how much you'll earn, or what others will think of you. The choice should be made strictly by an inward peace that only God can give you. We're told that God gives us the peace that passes all understanding (see Phil. 4:7). Only Jesus is the Prince of Peace. The enemy definitely cannot give you peace. Your spouse, your boss, your kids, and your pastor cannot give you peace—not the kind the Lord gives.

People sometimes ask me, "But what if I don't have that kind of peace yet, Pastor Johnny? What if I believe the Lord is calling me in this new direction, but I don't have peace about it yet?" To which I say, "Then wait on the Lord!" During such times of waiting, reflect on what the Psalmist provided us with—a good description of this attitude of the heart:

> I remain confident of this: I will see the goodness of the
>   LORD in the land of the living.
> *Wait for the LORD; be strong and take heart and wait for the*
>   *LORD.*
>
> —Psalm 27:13–14

The Psalmist also tells us, "Be still and know that I am God" (Ps. 46:10). Sometimes we simply must stand still. Be patient. Wait and see. Don't make a step before knowing God's timing and direction—and only God can give you peace about that. You can't make a choice based on what you think might happen. In fact, trying to jumpstart your future, even when you believe it's the future to which God is calling you, can sometimes backfire.

Just ask Joseph!

Playing Favorites

Perhaps no one illustrates how you can't jump ahead of God better than Joseph. He had a dream that his family bowed down to him and, in a moment of immaturity, rushed to tell his brothers. Now, Joseph was already disliked because his brothers knew that their little brother was their father Jacob's favorite.

They were envious of him. Jacob played favorites because Joseph was his son by Rachel, the woman he loved, not Leah, the woman he was tricked into marrying and whose sons were born out of obligation. Although Jacob likely loved his other children, he loved Joseph more. Jacob was drawn to his youngest son and did special things for him, which caused resentment in the family among Joseph's other siblings. When Joseph shared the dream he had, I wonder if he might have been trying to validate himself as important in the family: "I'm more than just my dad's son; I'm *somebody*. God has big plans for me. Just consider this dream I had!"

But here's the thing: we have to allow God to validate us. We don't try to validate ourselves to God. We've got to be assured of who we are. No matter what mistakes we have made or where we come from, or whatever our background or whatever our parents' background, we are validated through God. So we are not elevated or disqualified simply because of the things that have happened, good or bad, for us. The Scripture tells us that all things work for the good of those who love the Lord (Rom. 8:28).

Did God ordain Joseph to go to the pit? Was it His best choice for Joseph? No. But God will allow things to come into your life that you may think will destroy you, but that will build you and shift your attention from yourself to Him. And I've learned that over time, no matter what the situation is or how tough it gets, I must realize that God is in control. Is that an easy thing to do? No. But you've got to make yourself do it.

You've got to have the mind of Christ in every situation and remember that choices matter. Any choice that I make will affect my next generation, my lineage, and my legacy. That's why I go back to choices. You must *choose* to have God's peace.

We must learn to recognize the difference between things that are meant to encourage us in the moment and things that are meant to be quietly cultivated for future reference. Joseph wanted to be accepted by his brothers, but sharing something out of season affected the timing of the outcome. We should never share information out of our flesh to feed our weakness or build ourselves up. It will always backfire.

Another thing Joseph had to overcome was the generational curse of manipulation that ran in his family. His grandmother Rebekah played a part in this with his father, Jacob. The babies jostled each other within her, and she said, "Why is this happening to me?" So she went to inquire of the Lord. The Lord said to her, "Two nations are in your womb, and two peoples from within you will be separated; one people will be stronger than the other, and the older will serve the younger"

(Gen. 25:23). When the time came for her to give birth, there were twin boys in her womb. The first to come was red, and his whole body was like a hairy garment, so they named him Esau. After this, his brother came out with his hand grasping Esau's heel, so he was named Jacob. Isaac was sixty years old when Rebekah gave birth to them.

There are several things that stand out in this situation. One is that Rebekah attempted to help out based on what God told her when she inquired of Him. When we interfere or try to help something come to pass due to what God has told us, it will cause problems. Rebekah encouraged Jacob to deceive his father to receive the blessing that automatically fell on the firstborn. Rebekah interfered, which caused division between the brothers. Her intention was to assist God, but the Lord does not need our help, only our obedience. God watches over His Word to carry it out.

Our job is to obey Him. When things do not appear to be what God promised or they seem to be unfolding in a way we didn't expect, that's the time to trust and be still and know that He is God.

Intended for Good

Returning to the story of Joseph, after almost being murdered by his brothers who were angered by his dreams of greatness, Joseph became enslaved to foreigners—this time in Egypt. Despite such horrific circumstances—he could easily have blamed his family or God—Joseph remained faithful. He rose in the household of Potiphar, managing and leading with his natural intelligence, skill, and organizational mindset. Just as Joseph was on his way up, he faced false claims by his master's wife after scorning her seductive advances. So there he was, imprisoned for a crime he did not commit, once again without any logical hope or apparent resource—except his faith in God.

After successfully interpreting dreams for a fellow inmate, Joseph was brought before Pharaoh to interpret the troubling dream haunting his sleep. Not only did Joseph provide prophetic interpretation, but also he so impressed Pharaoh that the Egyptian leader appointed him second in command. Joseph was placed in charge of preparing for the upcoming famine as revealed in Pharaoh's dream. Joseph's managerial skills and savvy leadership flourished as he saved the bountiful harvests for the needs of the future.

Joseph's past and present collided, of course, when his brothers—the same ones who had left him in a pit to die, before reconsidering and selling him into slavery—came crawling from Israel and begging for food during the famine. After taunting them with the consequences of their past sinful actions, Joseph demonstrates his forgiveness and is reunited with his family in a joyful celebration. He knew that God had used all of the terrible circumstances of his life to orchestrate a divine elevation. Joseph said, "You intended to harm me, but God intended it for good to accomplish what is now being done, the saving of many lives" (Gen. 50:20).

Blessed by the Best

❋ No matter where you are or how you got there, no matter what you've suffered or how you've been overlooked, God has neither forgotten you nor abandoned you. He is working His good purposes through your willingness to step up and serve others. You may feel like just another employee number, just another voice in the choir, just another team member at the bottom of the organization, but you are first in God's eyes. You have been chosen by the Father to serve and to lead.

Before the Son of God ever began His public ministry, Jesus went to His cousin, John the Baptist, so He could be baptized in the Jordan River. Fully aware that He was God and was there in human form as the Messiah come to save us all from our sins, Christ obviously did not need to be baptized in order to be in a relationship with His Father or to serve the needs of His people. But in full humility and obedience, Jesus set an example for us all to follow. Even though He had yet performed no miracles, chosen no disciples, preached no sermons, Christ was baptized as a way of showing His acceptance of His Father's will. Jesus didn't have to perform, lead, heal, teach, feed, or forgive in order to please His Father. We're told, "As soon as Jesus was baptized, he went up out of the water. At that moment heaven was opened, and he saw the Spirit of God descending like a dove and alighting on him. And a voice from heaven said, 'This is my Son, whom I love; with him I am well pleased'" (Matt. 3:16–17).

Your Father is well pleased with you, too, my friend. He

has you in a position to leverage all that He has placed inside you. So don't worry, fret, or wallow in disappointment or discouragement. Your greatness will be revealed through your willingness to serve. You don't have to be up front, in charge, or at the top. God uses men and women behind the scenes, those following others, and those at the bottom of the organizational chart. You are chosen and blessed by God.

In His Sermon on the Mount (see Matt. 5–7), Jesus delivered what we know as the Beatitudes, in which He proclaimed that those who suffer, mourn, strive, and ache are blessed. These included the poor in spirit, the grief-stricken, the meek, the merciful, the peacemakers, and those who long for justice. Basically, Jesus turned the social order of His day upside down, likely surprising His listeners who were used to the rich, powerful, and politically connected being the ones who appeared to be blessed.

I wonder if we might consider that we, too, are blessed in roles that our culture might find less than admirable or desirable. Blessed are the waiters and waitresses, the maids and janitors, the gardeners and landscapers. Blessed are the sales reps and the customer service agents, the mid-level managers and the administrative assistants. Blessed are the character actors and associate pastors, the junior partners and assistant directors. Blessed are the second stringers, the benchwarmers, the relief pitchers, and understudies.

Blessed are all who are willing to serve their God by doing their best at all times. You have been chosen by your Father, and no matter your title or position, you are being used to achieve great purposes for His kingdom. It's time to look up, step up, and serve! You are blessed by the Best!

Your Next Step

1. When have you struggled to accept where God wanted you to serve? How did you respond? How has God used your struggle to equip you to step up?

2. Knowing that you are chosen by your Father to serve and to lead, what habits or practices do you need to change in order to be more effective in your current role?

※

Heavenly Father, I know You have ordained my steps and that You are with me each step I take. Forgive me for the times when I have grumbled or complained or disobeyed in an attempt to put myself first, in order to get ahead. Help me to trust Your timing and to know that Your purposes are always at work, no matter how circumstances might appear to me. I'm so grateful for Your blessing and I'm willing to step up and serve You wherever You lead me. Amen.

※

CHAPTER FIVE

Living in the Moment

"Time isn't the main thing. It's the only thing."
—MILES DAVIS

Not long after I joined the pastoral staff at Lakewood Church, Pastor John asked me to coordinate a conference call with several of our ministry partners around the country. I was delighted to do it and proceeded to email each leader, inquire as to their availability, and then set up a dial-in conference number on the selected date. When that day came, however, I discovered a major problem: I had not accounted for the various time zones for each participant. I had set the call for 10 a.m. but had not specified that this would be Central Time, our time zone in Houston. As a result, most callers assumed it was 10 a.m. in each of their respective time zones!

I learned a valuable lesson that day, and not just about paying attention to the details and making sure everyone knew the specific time for their time zone. More important, I learned that each of us assumes that our schedule is the center of everyone else's. Now, while most of us would deny it if someone asked, we often allow our schedule to reflect our status. If we're in an important role doing significant work, then we think our time is more valuable and others should recognize this. The problem, however, occurs when our different *personal* time zones collide. This means we have to learn a new way of viewing our schedule.

We have to switch to Eternal Standard Time!

Eternity in Our Hearts

If there's a secret to stepping up and becoming a more effective leader, it has to be living in the present moment. Each day presents new opportunities, and if you're stuck in the past or consumed by looking ahead at the future, then you will miss what the Lord puts in front of you today. You must adjust your way of spending time to reflect the only real time you have available—this present moment.

We frequently hear this message about living in the moment, but rarely does it seem to sink into our bones and become the rhythm of our life. But the older I get, the more I recognize that our days are numbered. God has allocated our lifetime and gives us each new day to spend in the joyful purpose for which He created us. Our job is to learn how to live in God's eternal time zone.

The Bible reminds us that God is the curator of our seasons in this life, even though He is beyond time as we know it. We're told, "He has made everything beautiful in its time. He has also set eternity in the human heart; yet no one can fathom what God has done from beginning to end" (Eccles. 3:11). And this reflects the paradox with which we must make peace if we want to make the most of our time: we are eternal spiritual beings housed in mortal, temporal bodies. Our spirits live forever even as our flesh is passing away. Consider how the Psalmist expresses both the finite and infinite aspects of our human experience:

> Show me, LORD, my life's end and the number of my days;
> let me know how fleeting my life is.
> You have made my days a mere handbreadth; the span
> of my years is as nothing before you. Everyone is but a
> breath, even those who seem secure.
> Surely everyone goes around like a mere phantom; in vain
> they rush about, heaping up wealth without knowing
> whose it will finally be.
> *But now, Lord, what do I look for? My hope is in you.*
>
> —Psalm 39:4–7

A breath. A vapor. A shadow passing over the withering grass. We have one life to step up and serve up all that God has placed inside us. One journey to make as we seek to follow God and serve those around us just as Jesus did. If you don't have time to do it right, when will you ever have time to do it over?

When you lose time, it can never be recovered.

We must use time wisely and realize that the time is always perfect to do our best and give our all. There is a particular patience that you have to develop to live in the moment. Jesus said, "But seek first his kingdom and his righteousness, and all these things will be given to you as well. Therefore do not worry about tomorrow, for tomorrow will worry about itself. Each day has enough trouble of its own" (Matt. 6:33–34). Notice what He is telling us here: when you put God first, then you don't have to worry about what happens next.

Basically, when you bring tomorrow's challenges and issues into today you only compound your day. When we do not live in the present, it makes today harder than it has to be. Some people like to challenge me on this by reminding me that God wants us to be prepared, to invest our talents wisely, and to work hard as a good and faithful servant. All of this is true, but none of it requires us to try and control how tomorrow will go. I fear too often we confuse preparation and wise investment with control and avoidance of problems and pain. We are not in control of events in this life—only God is sovereign and in control of everything, on earth and in heaven. We are, however, responsible to engage in the present and serve out of what we have been given. This news should liberate us to maximize our efforts!

Audit Your Time

※ If you're struggling to get as much done in your day as you believe you're capable of or if you already know there are ways to spend your time more wisely, then I encourage you to do a time audit. This is different from keeping a calendar or updating your appointments. A time audit requires you to jot down a word or phrase in reflection upon how you spent the hours in each day. I recommend keeping track of your time for at least one week in order to assess how you're managing your time.

Were you supposed to be writing a report for your committee when you ended up surfing the Internet for forty-five minutes? Did your lunch with a friend turn into a quick shopping trip? Did date night with your spouse become eating out while you both stared at your phones and responded to texts? Time audits are necessary to restore our perspective and refocus our time in light of our priorities. Seeing what consumes your minutes, hours, and days usually reveals where your heart is focused.

Jesus said, "For where your treasure is, there your heart will be also" (Matt. 6:21). We tend to define treasure here as our money and financial habits, which it indeed includes. But all the money in the world means nothing compared to the finite amount of time we have. Money comes and goes and can be replaced. We spend time and can never replace it. So in my thinking, Jesus' reference to treasure must include how we spend our time.

If your heart is focused on God and His kingdom, then you spend your precious time serving Him. If your relationship with God is your treasure, you will spend time reading His Word, living by His guidelines and principles, and serving others wherever He has led you. If you're focused only on making money, advancing your career, and serving your ego, then you will never live in the present moment. You will always be chasing something to increase what is incapable of satisfying your heart.

How you spend your free time can be especially revealing. Are you putting God first or are you putting yourself first? If you're focused on your appearance and what others think of you, then you may spend most of your time working out, shopping for designer clothes, and trying to look as youthful and attractive as possible. Keep in mind, it's good to pursue good health by eating well and exercising regularly. But when our appearance becomes our motivation, then we're not investing in eternity.

As you review your time audit, keep the truth in mind. Only God can fulfill you and satisfy your soul. Your time is limited. Your body will pass away. But you can invest in eternity by making the most of the moments you have.

Out of Time

When you're fully aware of how you're spending your time, then you can manage it more wisely. As your most precious asset, your time must be cherished, and that means being present for the moments in today. Every single thing you do requires time. Whether making a cup of coffee, writing a letter, sending a text, building a house, or starting a relationship, they all come at a price—some of your time.

While it may seem alarming to consider the brevity of our life here on earth, we have a God who is timeless. As we see in the Bible, God exists beyond the confinement and limitations of time as we know it. He is the Great I Am and has always been and will always be. He is part of the invisible spiritual realm of reality that is unique and distinct from our physical world and its dimensions. We're told that God is Spirit (see John 4:24) and therefore is not limited by the same laws of physics and dimensions of science known to us (see Isa. 57:15). It's one of those mind-stretching truths to consider that God, as the Creator, created time and yet is not subject to it.

As the Psalmist reminds us, God endures a timeless existence: "For a thousand years in Your sight are like a day that has just gone by, or like a watch in the night" (Ps. 90:4). While our human lives are limited and our bodies are passing away, God remains strong and unwavering in the face of time. Nonetheless, the Lord works within this gift of time to us and guides us through various seasons of life. Again, we're told, "There is a time for everything, and a season for every activity under the heavens" (Eccles. 3:1).

For many of us seeking to step up and serve as leaders, the challenge is often in recognizing the season we're in—especially as compared to the season we wish we were in! It's not that God doesn't want us dreaming and envisioning where we are going as we follow His call on our lives. It's simply that we have to balance our dreams with the requirements of each day, taking the next step toward our divine destiny.

Knocked Off Your Feet

✳ Maintaining this balance between dreaming and walking can be difficult during the trials and storms of life. It reminds me of when our children were very young and we would visit the beach. They would play and frolic in the sand and surf, laughing and running as the incoming waves washed over their feet. Only sometimes, the waves would be more powerful than they anticipated and knock them down. They would try to get up, only to be knocked down again by the current of the next wave. Often, my wife or I would have to intervene and lift them above the churning surf in order for them to regain their balance on solid ground.

In moments of crisis, we too often feel knocked down and battered by life's blows, unable to get back on our feet and regain the rhythm of our routines. During these times, I've learned to remain flexible and to look for what the Lord may be trying to teach me. It may simply be a time to rely more fully on Him and to allow Him to pick me up, much like I used to do with my own children at the seashore. Or it may be time to change my habits, to slow down or speed up the tempo of life, or to take time to focus on a particular area of need.

How do *you* usually respond when the waves of life knock you down? Do you remain on the ground and try to figure out what happened and how you can prevent it from happening again? Do you feel sorry for yourself and wait for someone to come along and pick you up? Do you wallow in the agony of life's unfairness? Do you analyze the situation in hopes of defending yourself for the next time?

Sometimes the unexpected arrival of such calamity leaves us disoriented and dazed. We feel paralyzed and don't know how we will ever move forward and get back on our feet. Other times, we react instantly and try to regain control of the situation as we seek higher ground. We frantically scamper and race to rectify and to resolve the crisis. But the only higher ground that can permanently secure our footing in such times is our faith in God.

You see, it's often your response in those moments of crisis that determines how you will make the most of your time. In addition to seeking God's help, you may be forced to ask for the assistance of others. You may be forced to slow down, take time off from work, recover from an injury, or take much needed personal time to plan, to grieve, or to regroup. If you want to make the most of your moments, then being attuned to God's guidance is essential.

Time and Time Again

How we respond to the moments of life each day can change the course of our existence. But the Bible refers primarily to two kinds of time, one that's familiar and one that requires more explanation. As we've seen, every person born into life on this planet is bound by time. This is time as we know it and it waits for no one. Seconds pass into minutes,

minutes into hours, then into days, weeks, months, and years. No matter who you are, rich or poor, young or old, struggling or succeeding, time encompasses all of us within its passage.

The Greek word *chronos* is often used when referring to this kind of linear, progressive, quantitative time. We see this word embedded in our own language in words like *synchronous, anachronism, chronological,* and *chronometer* (also known as a watch or clock!). In the Bible, we find *chronos* used when describing a length or passage of time (see Acts 1:7, Acts 13:18).

The second kind of time in Scripture is *kairos.* If chronos is about quantity of time, then kairos is about quality. Kairos refers to moments that present us with opportunities, with intersections, with the right time to do what we need to do. Such moments may appear to be coincidental, but for those of us who know the Lord, we recognize they are divinely appointed. Kairos reflects the season we're in and our alignment with God's timing. We see kairos in such passages as Luke 12:56, Romans 5:6, Galatians 6:9, and 1 Timothy 2:6.

Although they are more layered in their meanings, we might think about chronos as human time and kairos as God's time. Unfortunately, we often forget about keeping kairos time because we get so caught up in chronos time. We get too busy filling up our schedules that we miss the present moments where God reveals Himself and wants to point out His opportunities to us. Learning to step up and slow down means getting in sync with kairos and not just chronos. This requires us to be highly attuned to the prompting of the Holy Spirit and not just the alarm on our smart watch.

Running on kairos time often requires us to wait because kairos time runs on patience more than planning.

Hurry Up and Wait

�֎ We've all been in situations where we rush and scramble only to be forced to wait and wonder. Whether it's getting to the doctor's office or a television production, a business meeting or a miracle healing, we rush to where we know we must do things only to be sidelined and forced to wait. And when we cannot understand the delay, it becomes harder to wait. I'm convinced that, ultimately, patience requires faith.

This is the hard lesson some of Jesus' closest friends learned in one of their darkest moments. It happened when Jesus was in Jerusalem with His disciples when He received word that Lazarus, brother to Martha and Mary, had taken ill. Curiously enough, however, Jesus waited two more days before traveling to Bethany, where His beloved friends lived (see John 11:6). By the time He arrived, His friend had already died:

> On his arrival, Jesus found that Lazarus had already been in the tomb for four days. Now Bethany was less than two miles from Jerusalem, and many Jews had come to Martha and Mary to comfort them in the loss of their brother. When Martha heard that Jesus was coming, she went out to meet him, but Mary stayed at home.

"Lord," Martha said to Jesus, "if you had been here, my brother would not have died."

—John 11:17–21

Knowing everything because He is God, Jesus obviously knew when and how His friend would die. And Christ also knew that Lazarus's death was an opportunity for God's power and glory to be manifest: "It is for God's glory so that God's Son may be glorified through it" (John 11:4). But Martha and Mary respond as I suspect most of us would respond. They couldn't understand why Jesus waited when He could have come sooner and healed their brother's illness, saving his life.

Even when Jesus tries to explain that Lazarus will rise again, Martha assumes He is talking about the "resurrection at the last day" (John 11:24). Then Christ, after weeping and then praying to His Father, calls His friend Lazarus to come out of the tomb even though his deceased body had been contained there for four days. The dead man returns to life and emerges from the tomb still wrapped in the burial linens.

Too often we rely only on chronos time and assume that because we didn't get what we asked God to give us right away that He is ignoring us. We wait—two days, four days, a week, a month, or even years—and can't understand why the Lord is not intervening to provide the miracle, the provision, the healing we know He is more than capable of delivering. But this is where we must practice patience and adhere to kairos time. This waiting requires faith in the wisdom, character, goodness, and power of God.

Notice that when Jesus is discussing with Martha the timing of his arrival and Lazarus's death, He makes a much larger, timeless point: "I am the resurrection and the life. The one who believe in me will live, even though they die; and whoever lives by believing in me will never die. Do you believe this?" (John 11:25–26). Suddenly, the Lord shifted from the immediate situation of Lazarus's death to the power of death that is held over all of mankind.

But Jesus knew what was to come. He knew why He was on earth. With Christ's death on the cross for our sins and His resurrection to new life, He secured eternal life for all of us. Lazarus's death and resurrection only foreshadowed what Jesus would do on a cosmic scale.

Yes, Martha and Mary were absolutely correct: Jesus could have arrived sooner and healed their brother's body before it expired. But in God's divine wisdom and timing, Lazarus was allowed to die so that Jesus could reveal His power over death—both with Lazarus right then but also for all people with His own death on the cross and resurrection. Jesus allowed Mary and Martha to wait, to suffer, and to grieve before restoring their brother to new life. They didn't even consider such an option to be a possibility. But Jesus did and He knew God had appointed that moment for His glory to be revealed in a new way.

We must be willing to wait and, yes, sometimes to suffer and to grieve all while trusting that God's timing is divine. His sense of a chosen, appointed time will never conform to our clocks and calendars. Like the essence of His being, God's interaction with time remains mysterious and often unfathomable to us. What seems impossible to us is always possible for God. Any time we have lost and regrets we may have can never prevent God from blessing us and using us for His glory. We only have to step up and reset our hearts to kairos time.

Time of Your Life

As a pastor, I often have the privilege of walking with an individual or a family during someone's terminal illness. Whether the doctor's expectation for their lifespan is a matter of days, weeks, or months, the impact such news has on them is always the same. They experience the classic stages of grieving, including shock, denial, anger, hope, and acceptance. When you're forced to realize that you have only a limited supply of days, hours, and breaths left, then the passing of each one becomes urgently significant. You no longer have the luxury of ignoring your body's warning signs or your cognitive knowledge of mortality.

When these individuals know their days are literally numbered, then suddenly their priorities are crystal clear. They move from the shallow waters of self-awareness to the deep end of their own mortality. They know the tide is coming in and will carry them away very soon.

They know with whom they want to spend their precious remaining time. They know what they would like to do and what can be ignored or forgotten. They know whom they need to forgive and from whom they need to ask forgiveness. They know what needs to be said and what needs to go unsaid. They know when to laugh and when to cry. They know what business needs to be finished before the Lord takes them to heaven.

In all of these situations where I've walked with these people and their families, not one has wished they spent more time surfing the Internet, binge watching the latest online drama, or shopping for more shoes. Not one regrets the time spent with their children, and nearly all wish they had spent more of their time and attention on those they love.

We would all do well to heed this urgent sense of making the most of our moments. No one is guaranteed another day. Each one is a gift from the Lord. We should celebrate each as a new and precious treasure. "This is the day the Lord has made; we will rejoice and be glad in it" (Ps. 118:24, NKJV).

If you want to step up, then you have to pay attention to what and who is in front of you right now. You have to listen, to engage, and to hear with your heart. If you're thinking about what you forgot to do yesterday or need to prepare for tomorrow, then you overlook the joy set before you because each moment God gives us unfolds with opportunities to love, to lead, and to live for Him. We don't know how long we will be alive in our bodies on this side of heaven. We do know that we have been given today.

So don't waste it, my friend. Don't squander this precious gift. Pay attention to those you've been called to lead and to serve. Look at each moment as a chance to step up, to find some way to give all you've got. Let each day be a fresh start with a willing heart. Make the most of your moments while you still have moments to make!

Your Next Step

1. How would you describe your relationship with time at this point in your life? Never enough? Too much on your hands? Not enough for what matters most? Aware of the clock ticking on some important goal or dream? Something else?

2. What needs to change in order for you to make the most of the time God has given you? What time-wasters need to be eliminated? What moment-makers need to be practiced? How can you make the most of your moments as you step up?

Dear God, today is the day You have made for me so I will rejoice and be glad in it! I'm so grateful for my life and the time You have given me here on this earth. Help me to make the most of each day by trusting You to guide my steps. Let Your Holy Spirit keep me in the present moment, letting go of any regrets or disappointments from yesterday as well as any worries or anxious fears about tomorrow. Even as I move through chronos time, Lord, keep my heart aligned with kairos and Your perfect sense of timing. May I make the most of my moments and make a difference for eternity.

Amen.

CHAPTER SIX

No Strings Attached

"If selfishness is the key to being miserable, then selflessness must be the key to being happy!"
—Joyce Meyer

The young man looked at me through bloodshot, tearful eyes. After arranging to meet with me privately, he had poured out his story, perhaps for the first time, about the impact his fast-and-loose lifestyle was having on his heart. At first it was just drinking and clubbing every weekend, but then he began hooking up with young women on a regular basis. Like many of his generation, he had become accustomed to meeting young ladies online, exchanging pictures and flirting via text, and then meeting for a quick, no-strings-attached encounter. As he had discovered, however, there *were* strings attached.

As I explained to him, it's practically impossible to compartmentalize the gift of our sexuality apart from our emotions. Like cobwebs clinging to the rafters of his soul, he found that these impersonal, transactional encounters with others had left him cold, disappointed, and frustrated. Despite the physical closeness, he surprised himself by longing for an emotional connection and human intimacy. I explained that because our bodies house our souls, God intends for us to reserve physical intimacy for the commitment of marriage. Commitment means there are strings attached, vows that exclude each spouse from sharing themselves with anyone else.

He knew what he had done was wrong so I didn't criticize or condemn his past actions. Instead I talked about God's forgiveness of sins, the free gift of grace imparted to us by Christ's death on the cross, and the new life of joy, purpose, and contentment we can experience when we walk in the power of the Holy Spirit. Basically, I used this opportunity to describe the only relationship that truly has no strings attached—our relationship with God.

Powered by Love, Fueled by Freedom

Our human relationships, whether in the bedroom or the boardroom, always have strings attached—unless we're motivated by God's love and not our own. The only way to step up and serve unconditionally is to have your needs met by God and to live according to His guidelines. To obey His commands and to follow the direction of His Holy Spirit dwelling within you, not out of obligation, guilt, or a sense of duty—but motivated by love, devotion, and a desire to serve.

Because we human beings have a natural tendency to put ourselves first, we can only experience this motivation supernaturally. The Bible tells us that the only reason we can love others is because we know the true source of all love—God:

> We love because he first loved us. Whoever claims to love God yet hates a brother or sister is a liar. For whoever does not love their brother and sister, whom they have seen, cannot love God, whom they have not seen. And he has given us this command: Anyone who loves God must also love their brother and sister.
>
> —1 John 4:19–21

When you stop and think about it, the fact that God loves us does not make sense—not any logical, rational sense. For one thing, God does not need us, at least not in the way that we might think of someone needing something from us. He's the all-powerful, all-knowing Almighty God, the Great I Am, the Creator of heaven and earth and everything that exists. God does not need our physical strength, our mental prowess, or our emotional comfort. He exists in perfect holiness. We, on the other hand, are selfish, sinful, and incapable of atoning for our imperfections.

And yet . . . God loves *us*.

He doesn't even need our love, but He loves us as His children and wants to be in relationship with us. In fact, He loves us so much that He gave up His most precious Son to die for us. Here's how Paul explains this curious fact in his letter to the Christians in Rome: "Very rarely will anyone die for a righteous person, though for a good person someone might possibly dare to die. But God demonstrates His own love for us in this verse: 'While we were still sinners, Christ died for us'" (Rom. 5:7–8).

All we have to do is accept this free gift. All we need to do is embrace His grace. Because when we do, then we experience the freedom that comes from walking in the power of the Spirit. And it's this freedom and this power that fuels our ability to lead and serve selflessly. In every occasion, we can find an opportunity to serve and be a blessing to those around us—if we're doing it freely and selflessly without expecting anything in return. Only when we're fueled by the freedom we have in Christ can we serve at maximum capacity, reaching heights that we could never scale in our own power.

Strings Create Snares

When we attach strings to our service, we create traps that ensnare us as well as those we seek to serve. When we try to anticipate their response and how to give them what they want, we're actually seeking to get what we want—attention, appreciation, and affirmation. We end up looking for others to reward us or bless us when it's not their responsibility to do so.

When we're motivated by what we can get from others, the traps we create cut us on both sides. If we get the praise and pats on the back we crave, then we're likely to keep relating this way. When others notice our service and stroke our egos, then we only want more. On the other hand, if others don't give us the attention we hoped to receive, then our disappointment can become bitterness.

In either direction, we're not able to give to our full capacity as God created us to serve. Only when we are motivated by pleasing God can we hope to escape this performance trap. The Bible tells us, "Whatever you do, work at it with all your heart, as working for the Lord, not for human masters, since you know that you will receive an inheritance from the Lord as a reward. It is the Lord Christ you are serving" (Col. 3:23–24). Clearly, we are not to allow human recognition, material gain, or popular opinion to motivate our work.

In his letter to the early church in Galatia, Paul addressed this problem head on. Apparently, some people there had started to preach based on what they thought others wanted to hear. Rather than teach the truth of the Gospel, these teachers tickled the ears of their listeners in order to gain popularity and influence. In order to combat this problem, Paul gave them a way to test their motives: "Am I now trying to win the approval of human beings, or of God? Or am I trying to please people? If I were still trying to please people, I would not be a servant of Christ" (Gal. 1:10).

God is fully aware of your service and sacrifice, and He is keeping account of every seed you plant, every branch you prune, and every fruit you produce. We're told that we must step out and serve in faith as we earnestly seek God's approval, not the approval of men and women: "And without faith it is impossible to please God, because anyone who comes to him must believe that he exists and that he rewards those who earnestly seek him" (Heb. 11:6).

We should not grow weary or get tired of doing what is right. When you serve with a humble, devoted heart, you will be motivated to continue doing what God has called you to do—whether others notice it or not. When you look for validation and affirmation from another person, you may not get noticed. And even if you do, someone else may not be able to fully appreciate the diligence, hard work, and sacrifice that went into your service.

The ancient Romans developed a phrase we still use today to describe this kind of approach in which we give in order to receive: *quid pro quo*, literally meaning "something for something." When I was growing up, I heard another version of this same expression that you might know as well—"You scratch my back and I'll scratch yours." No matter what we call it, though, this way of thinking always sets you up for disappointment and poisons your attitude and behavior.

It's like giving your spouse a gift and then expecting a

certain reaction because of what you've given. Once they receive it and for whatever reason do not respond as you had hoped, then you become upset, disappointed, or angry. You think, "Don't they know how much that gift cost? Doesn't she realize how long I've been saving for this? Doesn't he see what I had to give up to share this?"

But, again, this is the wrong motivation—it's basically manipulation veiled in false, sacrificial service. In giving, you must ask yourself, *"Did I do it to make me happy? Or did I do it to make them happy? Or did I do it to please the Lord?"* When we expect things in return, it always leads to frustration and disappointment. Set your mind to this: "I am here to please God and not other people."

If you please God, you will automatically please others who are attuned to His Spirit. You don't have to force relationships or contrive connections to create such bonds. You naturally become a blessing in each other's lives. Organic connections, those that happen naturally as a result of each person putting God first, typically develop into healthy growth.

When an athlete takes some performance-enhancing drugs, the muscle grows faster and bigger, but there are a lot of negative side effects. Manipulated connections force unnatural events to occur because we're motivated by our fleshly desires to get ahead. And when one person begins being motivated selfishly, it can quickly spread like a cancer that undermines shared goals. Each person focuses only on themselves instead of what God wants.

Your motivation to serve or help someone should be pure.

Don't go into service thinking that if you help someone they will give you opportunities to establish yourself. Do not use any connection or position as an opportunity to promote yourself or ideas—that's not the way to step up.

Instead, use your connections and positions of leadership as opportunities for service to God. Use them as occasions to draw closer to God and to more fully discover all He has placed within you. Use them as moments to rely on His Spirit to guide and direct you. When the Lord is your power source, you will never need strings to fly! It's the difference between being Superman or Wonder Woman, soaring with no strings attached, and acting as a stage play character like Peter Pan, who flies only through the support of wires and pulleys. God empowers us to step up and serve like superheroes—not puppets on a string!

The First Must Be Last

When we stop relying on God for our power, however, our attitude and behavior have a domino effect throughout the areas where we serve. When we're motivated by showing off our abilities, talents, and blessings, then we risk our contribution backfiring. Instead of helping and blessing others, we end up undermining the entire focus of our team, ministry, or organization.

This kind of "look at me" attitude often emerges in sports. I grew up loving the big three, as we called them: football, basketball, and baseball. What I loved about playing each of these is the way the team's success relied on the collective talent of each individual being shared together for the common goal of winning the competition. The old coach's cliché that *there's no "I" in "team"* proved true time and time again. Players, especially the ones who were extraordinary in their athletic talent and natural gifting, could easily focus only on their own performance.

Often, the star quarterback, the all-pro forward, and the homerun slugger would be motivated by showing off their ability as they carried the team to victory. Only, one person cannot make a team. Showboats often end up on a sinking ship! If everyone else feels like their role is only to showcase the star's talent, it takes away the fun of the game, the shared camaraderie, that sense of each player being stretched to do their best by the commitment to their other team members. Relying on the talent of only one person destroys the unity required for remarkable achievements because depending on a showboat to power the team often becomes one player paddling his own rowboat!

This dynamic is not limited to athletic fields and basketball courts. You can find it in virtually any group endeavor—including the church. Even in Jesus' day, this ego-based competitive spirit rose up among His own disciples. And the jockeying for power positions took a surprising turn, as we see in this encounter Jesus had with the mother of two of his disciples:

Then the mother of Zebedee's sons came to Jesus with her sons and, kneeling down, asked a favor of him.

"What is it you want?" he asked.

She said, "Grant that one of these two sons of mine may sit at your right and the other at your left in your kingdom."

"You don't know what you are asking," Jesus said to them. "Can you drink the cup I am going to drink?"

"We can," they answered.

Jesus said to them, "You will indeed drink from my cup, but to sit at my right or left is not for me to grant. These places belong to those for whom they have been prepared by my Father."

When the ten heard about this, they were indignant with the two brothers. Jesus called them together and said, "You know that the rulers of the Gentiles lord it over them, and their high officials exercise authority over them. Not so with you. Instead, whoever wants to become great among you must be your servant, and whoever wants to be first must be your slave—just as the Son of Man did not come to be served, but to serve, and to give his life as a ransom for many."

—Matthew 20:20–28

Now you know the competition is fierce when someone's mama gets involved! It's like a parent coming to their children's teacher and saying, "Won't you let my little darlings have the best parts in the school play? They're so talented! I just know you'll be glad you picked them." Forgive me for the comparison, but I think you know what I'm talking about. As parents, we want the best for our kids, and the mother of James and John was no different.

Notice how Jesus responded, though, and how quickly James and John piped up to make their case (maybe they asked mama to intervene!). The Master tells them that they have no idea what they're asking. In other words, if you want the kind of position for which you're asking, then it comes at a high price of sacrifice, service, and suffering. When the brothers assure Jesus that they're up for the challenge, the Lord tells them that only His Father can award such roles.

Meanwhile, this entire conversation ignites a quarrel among the rest of the disciples who don't think it's fair that James and John should get any kind of privileged position. The others want their fair share and want to be noticed, appreciated, and rewarded for their commitment to Christ. But then Jesus reminds them that He's not going to set up an earthly kingdom like they might expect in light of the Roman Empire's conquest of Israel. Jesus said, "Instead, whoever wants to become *great* among you must be your *servant*, and whoever wants to be *first* must be your *slave*—just as the Son of Man did not come to be served, but to serve" (Matt. 20:26–28, my emphasis).

When you're worried about where you stand in the pecking order of an organization, then you're always going to be worried about others getting ahead of you. Your mindset becomes one of competition and not collaboration. Jesus' disciples seemed to struggle with this mindset as well because they were not only jealous of one another but of others they saw ministering:

> An argument started among the disciples as to which of them would be the greatest. Jesus, knowing their thoughts, took a little child and had him stand beside him. Then he said to them, "Whoever welcomes this little child in my name welcomes me; and whoever welcomes me welcomes the one who sent me. For it is the one who is least among you all who is the greatest."
>
> "Master," said John, "we saw someone driving out demons in your name and we tried to stop him, because he is not one of us."
>
> "Do not stop him," Jesus said, "for whoever is not against you is for you."
>
> —Luke 9:46–50

Not One but Many

When we are motivated by our relationship with God, then we can make our unique contribution humbly without jealousy, competition, or envy. We can then appreciate the contributions others make without worrying about whether our role is as important as theirs. We can trust that all parts of the team are necessary to work in harmony and to achieve shared goals.

This is the dynamic we're told should guide our relationships with other believers. Members of the early church were no different than any other human beings who lived before them or after them. They began feeling overlooked and grew jealous of one another. It's the same thing we still experience today, whether it be the choir member secretly seething over the selection for soloist or the businessman trying to give more than others in his small group. But we are each created for unique and undeniable roles in God's kingdom. We can only serve as one whole Body of Christ when we respect the need for many parts:

> Just as a body, though one, has many parts, but all its many parts form one body, so it is with Christ. For we were all baptized by one Spirit so as to form one body—whether Jews or Gentiles, slave or free—and we were all given the one Spirit to drink. Even so the body is not made up of one part but of many.
> —1 Corinthians 12:12–14

1 Corinthians says that no part is too small or too trivial (21–24)! Each one of us contributes something indispensable to the kingdom of God. So often in the business world we're told to remember that everyone can be replaced, that no matter how important any employees seems to think they are, the organization can survive—if not thrive—without them. But in the Body of Christ, we are all equally valuable contributors.

No one is more important than anyone else. What I do is no less important than what Joel does. What the parking attendants for our services do is no less important than what I do. We all serve together as God has designed and equipped us to serve. We are each indispensable!

A Lasting Legacy

✾ I start my day by asking God to reveal to me what I need to do regarding everything that may come my way. As His Word said, "Lean not on your own understanding; in all your ways acknowledge Him, and He shall direct your paths" (Prov. 3:6, NKJV). Basically that means you are giving God permission to participate in your every decision and every move—instead of being guided by what you think will be in your own best interest. You must always remind yourself that He is the only one who gives the orders that are truly for your best interests.

God gets involved by invitation only, which is why we must remember that only His will works to guide us and help us step up. Nothing can change or defeat His will and His plan. So that is why it is so important for us to pray and get His plan for every situation in our life. This daily gut check through prayer can help us guard ourselves from getting jealous or competitive with the ones we serve.

One example in the Bible is the relationship between Jonathan and David. Jonathan was the son of King Saul, so therefore he was next in line to become the king of Israel. Only that is not what God had planned. God called Jonathan to step up and serve David by stepping down from his right to claim his father's throne. Because Jonathan and David had surrendered their own will to God, the two men became the best of friends. They loved each other as brothers. On the other hand, King Saul became increasingly jealous of David, viewing him as a threat to Saul's own identity and royal role to the point that Saul tried to kill David (for the full story, see 1 Sam. 18 and following).

Jonathan started serving David with no strings attached instead of clinging to the traditional entitlement that Jonathan could have maintained. His heart was knit with David's, and they enjoyed a covenant relationship based on trust and respect. By loving and serving David, Jonathan created a legacy that was blessed by his obedience and willingness to serve as God called him to serve. Mephibosheth, Jonathan's son, was restored and blessed in the royal house of King David because of his father, Jonathan.

Similarly, although you might not see it all come to pass in your lifetime, future generations might receive blessings from your acts of kindness and service. When you give of yourself faithfully, you might not receive the reward, but your offspring and generations to come can look forward to it because of your service.

Too often the world in which we live revolves around the question, "What can you do for me?" Everybody's looking for the angle that will benefit them without regard for the impact of their actions upon others, let alone what God might want them to do instead. But the Bible says it is more blessed to give than to receive (see Acts 20:35). A lot of people forget about that very important principle of life. They end up frustrated because they can never have enough—be it money, fame, or accolades. Only when we serve with no strings attached can we receive the only reward—God's reward—that will satisfy our soul.

Your Next Step

1. When have you experienced situations or relationships with strings attached? How did such strings affect your ability to step up as you know God wants you to serve? How can you avoid serving with strings attached in your present leadership roles?

2. When have you felt noticed, appreciated, and valued for your service by other people? When have you experienced the pleasure of the Lord from your willingness to serve Him first? How do the two compare?

Heavenly Father, I marvel at how You first loved me even when I was separated from You by my sin. Thank You for the gift of salvation through the gift of Your Son, Jesus. Thank You for the freedom I have to live by the power of Your Spirit and to be a servant leader. Cut any strings that my ego, pride, or insecurity might be tempted to attach to my relationships and acts of service. Remind me that what I have to contribute to those around me is unique, special, and indispensable to You and to Your kingdom. Allow me to give my best without trying to compare and compete with others, trusting that the reward You have for me is far better than anything this world can offer.

Amen.

CHAPTER SEVEN

Anchor Your Attitude

"I can't change the direction of the wind, but I can adjust my sails to always reach my destination."
—JIMMY DEAN

I f you want to step up, then your attitude serves as your anchor.

When you're in a position of leadership, you will often face obstacles, conflicts, and problems that seem too big to handle. When storms rage around you, you may fear being blown away. When the unexpected, the unimaginable, and the unpreventable event happens, you may not think you're capable of doing what's required in that situation. You might feel in over your head or like a fraud who will finally be exposed as incompetent, afraid, and uncertain. Perhaps as a leader, you feel insecure about your abilities, experience, or education. At times, others might assume you're not up to the task and proceed to communicate their opinion, either directly or indirectly.

The transition from the construction site to the church sanctuary certainly stretched my abilities, as well as the way I saw myself. When I was a young man building houses with my father, I focused more on the physical skills and technical abilities required to construct the structure at hand. I learned how to mix concrete, lay a foundation, and frame walls. Installing the electrical and plumbing systems became part of my contractor's education. My father was the boss, and although I occasionally supervised other workers or subcontractors, I wasn't required to have any management skills or emotional intelligence in my dealings with the people around me.

When I began volunteering at Lakewood, I mostly served in areas that were also more technical and mechanical in nature. As the Lord began to call me to preach and to serve on the pastoral team, I thought there must be some mistake. Up until that time, all my experience, both personal and professional, had little to do with being a pastor—or so it seemed. Pastors not only preach the Word, but they also minister and counsel their congregation and individuals in need. I thought of myself more as someone to remain behind the scenes.

However, as I began to sense God calling me into a new direction, I quickly realized that, although I might not have the experience I assumed one needed to pastor, I did have the right attitude—one dependent upon God, intent on pleasing Him, and geared toward serving others no matter what I was doing. I'm far from perfect, and like anyone else, I can occasionally let negative moods derail my focus, but I suspect it was my attitude of service that first attracted Pastor John's attention. He recognized that I was teachable, willing, and able to learn through obedience, hard work, and risk taking.

Attitude in Action

❋ So many servant leaders in the Bible came from obscurity and didn't necessarily see themselves as worthy of the roles in which God placed them. Abraham struggled to believe God would keep His promise to provide a son to him and his wife, Sarah, who would then become the beginning of a great nation. Moses tried to refuse God at the burning bush and came up with multiple excuses that were no good. Joseph believed God had chosen him for great things only to find himself sold by his brothers into slavery in a foreign country. He was then falsely imprisoned for doing the right thing in resisting the seductive advances of his master's wife. David, anointed by God to be the king of Israel, was merely a shepherd boy. Rahab was a prostitute, and Ruth was a poor widow from a foreign country. Both would become ancestors of Jesus mentioned in Matthew's genealogy of Christ.

The New Testament is no different. Jesus selected fishermen and tax collectors to be His disciples, not wealthy aristocrats or Jewish religious leaders. Paul, the apostle who preached the Gospel to the Gentiles and penned many of the divinely inspired epistles included in the Bible, had been a zealous bounty hunter intent on killing Christians before he met Jesus on the road to Damascus. On and on, time after time, it's clear that God enjoys using underdogs to become unlikely heroes of the faith. He doesn't need the most talented, most qualified, most educated, best looking, or most experienced.

God wants those who are willing to step up—people willing to surrender their own plans and preferences in order to serve God and fulfill their divine purpose. I doubt that the attitudes of those I mention from the Bible were always elevated and ethereal. In fact, we *know* some of them complained and doubted what God was doing, just like we all do sometimes. Many of the Psalmists express fear, anxiety, concern, and doubt—not to mention what we read by the authors of Lamentations, Ecclesiastes, and Job. But no matter what they faced, these men and women persevered and kept following God as instructed. And I can't help but believe that, along the way, they learned it didn't matter how they felt—as long as they lived by faith, which is basically your God-focused attitude in action.

Attitude Adjustment

When young leaders approach me, they often want to discuss how to adjust their attitudes, particularly toward their superiors. "How can I continue to serve and keep a positive attitude if I don't agree with the direction my boss is going?"

they ask. "What do I do when my frustration feels more powerful than my faith?"

First, I tell them that I understand their dilemma and can appreciate the challenge of maintaining the right attitude in a situation that feels wrong from their point of view. But then I remind them of three important variables that can often help them realign their attitudes with their trust in God based on one of my favorite verses of Scripture: "And now these three remain: faith, hope and love. But the greatest of these is love" (1 Cor. 13:13).

Number one, when our attitudes slip or we begin to succumb to feelings based on circumstances, then we have to walk by faith. And faith requires us to look beyond what we can see and how we feel: "Now faith is confidence in what we hope for and assurance about what we do not see" (Heb. 11:1). Notice what I consider the key word here—*confidence*. Even if we don't have confidence in our leader, supervisor, or boss, do we have confidence in trusting that God has us in that role for a reason? If not, then I suggest it's time to seek God's guidance about where He does in fact want you. If so, then I encourage you to keep going, day by day, step by step, holding onto him—not your feelings about your boss or the boss's feelings about you.

The second variable impacting our attitude is hope—the assurance of knowing what is true despite what we may see or what we can't see. Where does your assurance come from? Is it the result of job security, your employment contract, your friend in human resources, or your 401(k)? No, of course not! The Psalmist tells us, "We wait in hope for the Lord; he is our help and our shield. In him our hearts rejoice, for we trust in his holy name" (Ps. 33:20–21). I like the way our hope here is connected to the fact that God is our help and our shield, our provider and our protector. When our attitudes suffer, we can cling to hope in God to lift the burden on our hearts. He will continue to empower us and to protect us no matter what!

Finally, the third factor that can dramatically influence our attitudes is love. Of the three factors, we're told love is the greatest (see 1 Cor. 13:13). Just as you can love your spouse or your children and still disagree with them, so you can also love your leader even if you don't like his or her direction. Love has power both to open up honest conversation about issues on which we may disagree with others and to enable obedience even when our mind may not understand. I'm not advocating blind obedience here, especially if you're not confident in your supervisor's relationship with God, but I am encouraging you to demonstrate your love for God and for other people by seeking harmony rather than disharmony.

I love music of every kind, and our worship and praise music at Lakewood never fails to lift my heart and help my soul rejoice in the Lord. Because I'm often at the church or have to arrive there early, I frequently get to hear our musicians, singers, and worship leaders rehearsing. While they always sound better than I would, sometimes it's clear that something's not right. It might be an instrument out of tune, a singer just a little flat, or a tech problem with amplification or volume.

But in such moments, what I've witnessed is a community spirit of problem solving and a shared commitment to excellence. No one wants to sound bad up there, but when something's not right, they don't develop a negative attitude or try to shift blame. Instead, they work together to identify the problem, solve it, and continue practicing to be their best. No one tries to be a diva or refuses to continue the rehearsal. These people love the Lord and one another, and they love sharing their gifts with the rest of the Body of Christ during our services.

This is the kind of love we must practice when our tempers flare, our bodies lag, or our hearts feel overwhelmed. Love endures and suffers. It doesn't complain or brag or sow dissension. Love keeps trying, remains patient, shares everything, and never gives up. Too often, when negative emotions bubble up within us, we assume that they have power to influence our attitudes. While we can't control our emotions, we can limit the impact and influence they have on our attitudes. Our attitudes often serve to express what we feel, but more importantly, they have the power to express how we want to feel. Attitudes communicate the posture of our hearts. Emotions are like weather and will change throughout our day, but they need not change our attitude if we keep our hearts fixed on God.

Perseverance Outlasts Persecution

✳ Another way we can keep our attitudes in check as we seek to step up and serve others is by showing compassion and practicing empathy. Please understand that empathy is not sympathy. When we empathize with someone, we imagine what it's like to walk a mile in their shoes, as my daddy used to say. We see ourselves in their life, within their circumstances, and facing their challenges. Thus, our ability to identify with them is conveyed by our attitude and actions toward them.

Sympathy, on the other hand, may help us identify with someone's pain and suffering, but it distances us from any sadness or compassion we might feel. Offering someone sympathy usually implies a sense of gratitude that we are not in their shoes! In other words, we see their plight and we're glad we don't have to fight the battles they're called to fight. We're relieved and grateful not to be that person. Ultimately, I believe empathy extends your attitude toward serving others while sympathy raises the drawbridge as you seek to protect yourself, either consciously or subconsciously, from entering into others' pain.

This distinction has an important influence on your attitude, which of course impacts your ability to serve others well as you step up in your God-appointed roles. Lack of understanding someone else's point of view usually produces a bad attitude. You must first try to understand why someone does what he or she does. Think of it as giving someone directions to your home. The very first thing you try to establish when giving someone directions is knowing where they're starting. You must pinpoint their exact location in order to get them to their desired location: where you are.

Your true inward feelings will always reflect in your countenance and attitude. In your expressions, people can see the real you. Your thoughts feed your emotions, which will affect your attitude and behavior. Choose to think positively and your day will go much smoother. Paul gave members of the early church the same reminder we still need to hear today: "Finally, brothers and sisters, whatever is true, whatever is noble, whatever is right, whatever is pure, whatever is lovely, whatever is admirable—if anything is excellent or praiseworthy—think about such things" (Phil. 4:8).

In difficult times, it especially matters what you think. Right thinking will lead you out of tight squeezes and into the light of God's truth. You will step up and grow from opposition or pressure from external sources if—and it's often a big if—you can adjust your attitude and keep it from crashing in the storms of life. Or think about lifting weights—your muscles grow through the resistance of weight and pressure. When you first start working out, you become very sore. But if you continue the process and keep working out, the soreness will eventually dissipate as you become stronger and stronger.

Work through your season of soreness because it will soon end. Of all the saints I mentioned earlier, Joseph remains my favorite example of keeping the right attitude in seasons of growth. When Joseph was in prison, he had to have the right attitude because he was operating in his anointing even while suffering discomfort and injustice. His life provides a living testimony to the fact that perseverance will always outlast persecution. He is the epitome of the truth that God puts no limitation on faith, and faith puts no limitation on God. Joseph is proof that God can take things meant for evil and use them for good.

Even problems that may run from generation to generation cannot prevent you from fulfilling your divine destiny unless you choose to live under the curse instead of breaking it through the power of Christ in you. And the power of Christ in you comes through in your daily attitude. You must remember that you are redeemed from the curse of the law by Jesus Christ (see Gal. 3:13). Joel has shared many times about the spirit of poverty that presided over previous generations of his family and how his father, Pastor John, was determined to break it through the power of Jesus—and he did!

The same power is available for you and me, my friend.

Perseverance always outlasts persecution—always!

Identity and Integrity

If it's raining, I know I need an umbrella when I leave the house that morning. No one has to tell me I need an umbrella—not my wife or the weather anchor or anyone else. Similarly, God has already equipped you in certain ways that you should embrace without question or consideration. He said with man some things are possible, but with God all things are possible. So God expects you to do the possible. To do your part and to take the next step.

God has given you that ability. You were created in His image. We are created beings. If it's raining outside, why do you or I need to pray and ask God whether we should take our umbrella or not? That's foolishness! God has given you the ability to do so many things and to be resourceful and creative. So trust God even as you use the resources, gifts, and blessings that He's already poured into your life. Using what He's given you allows you to see how God can accomplish the impossible if you're willing to simply do what's possible. Do what's within your realm and allow God to do what's within His.

If you want to anchor a strong, positive attitude, you must also follow through with your word. Passion is supported by your integrity, your character, your attitude, and your word, and whatever you're passionate about will be sustained. Will you ever lose your passion entirely? No. Will you fall short some days? Yes, you will, but you have to be a person of integrity, someone willing to do the right thing, to obey God no matter who else might be looking at your life.

When I was growing up, I would do the right thing because my father was there. Even working with Pastor Joel, I always do the right thing because I know he is there. But I've learned to remind myself that I'm not simply serving my father or my pastor or the members of our church. Above all else, I'm serving God—so it doesn't matter who's looking over my shoulder or not.

Here's a small, somewhat funny example. My boss is a sharp dresser and meticulous about taking care of his suits and dress clothes. He hangs his suits very carefully, making sure that the pants are straight and the suit coat shoulders are perfectly aligned. He doesn't like putting his dress shirt over the pants and under the coat on a hanger because it can easily wrinkle. So shirts get a separate hanger. Belts, ties, and shoes also have their proper place. Occasionally, if our schedule is really tight or changes suddenly, I will need to pack up for Pastor Joel. Although I don't have to hang his suits and pack like he does, I do it because I know it pleases him. He's never commented on it and probably has never thought about it—which is my intention in packing the way he would.

Even something as simple as this example forces me to consider what motivates me. Am I striving to have integrity and do everything with excellence unto the Lord? Or am I doing it to win points with Pastor Joel or to hope he'll notice and commend me? We truly operate in integrity when those who matter most to us are not around. Because God is always present. So, I do the same thing regardless of who is watching because I know God is watching.

If you operate in this attitude, your ability to lead, to serve, and to step up will surprise you. God can bless integrity. Integrity produces obedience, which naturally yields the fruit of abundance. You don't have to work for specific beneficial outcomes because they will occur naturally. So why not just do the right thing regardless of what people might say!

Others will always offer their opinions and try to influence you to do what they would do, the way they would do it—instead of what God calls you to do with integrity. Don't let other people make you lay down your principles. Stick to your principles. Focus on what you're called to and where you're called to go—not on other people and their destination. For all you know, they might be a turkey while you're an eagle! Eagles soar high! If you're trying to hang out with the turkeys, you can't soar high. You can't reach the thermal winds. You have to realize who you are, who God made you to be, and to remain true to your identity.

If you watch an eagle, you very seldom see an eagle flapping his wings. Once he reaches a certain height, he just soars. As you take off and begin your career or ministry, the work might force you to do a whole lot of flapping. But rest assured you're going to keep climbing, and as you keep climbing, you're going to soar. The Bible tells us, "But those who hope in the LORD will renew their strength. They will soar on wings like eagles; they will run and not grow weary, they will walk and not be faint" (Isa. 40:31). God wants you to soar—and he will use the wind to blow you where you need to go.

An Anchor—and a Lifeline

❀ The key to anchoring your attitude is just staying focused and realizing who you are. Don't disqualify yourself because you were once hanging out with some chickens or turkeys. That's where the grace of God comes in! Don't look behind you or below you—look up and ahead. Stay focused on God's guidance. Don't disqualify yourself by your past or what people say to you, because if you do, then you will eventually disqualify yourself. But God has qualified you! You are his workmanship. You are a work in progress. You just have to stay focused and understand that your attitude can anchor you in the storms of life if you're tethered to the Rock of Ages.

Be reliable and trustworthy so that others can see that your attitude provides an anchor and a lifeline for them as well. If you say you're going to do something, then do it. Be a person of your word. Your word is almost as important as your name! When Pastor Joel asks me to go somewhere, if I say "yes," then I mean *yes*. He can rely on it. I give him my word.

Your track record and reliability inform your attitude. In fact, they also determine your attitude. When you're dealing with people and have discernment, when you have the right attitude, then it manifests in your expressions, your body language, and your relational style. Attitude may be invisible and internal, but it will show on your face. You will show it in your countenance.

You've likely seen this in others. They say nothing's wrong, but you can tell they're upset or angry by the way they deliver their words, raise their eyebrows, and cross their arms. The signs are all there for you and others to see. So when your attitude is not right, people see that. You can't hide it. People see it and you can't fake a right attitude.

So, let others see the love of Jesus in your attitude—in your smile, in your patience, in your humor, in your kindness, in your compassion, and in your attention to details. Try to be a blessing to them whether or not they are going to be a blessing to you. I get up in the morning and say, "God, how can I show Your love to someone today? Please use me to bless someone who needs to know Your love and kindness today." As corny as it may sound, I love serving others! I feel blessed and experience joy because I know I'm doing what God wants me to do, what He created me to do.

Serving is key to success. I can't stress it enough: Jesus said that He didn't come to be served but that He came to serve. A lot of people think serving is a degrading, burdensome obligation. They say, "I don't want to serve. I'm entitled. I am the head worship leader. I am the head usher. I am the pastor. Others need to recognize my position and serve me." No. If Jesus, who is the Son of God and who can raise the dead and walk on water, came to serve, then who are we to say we can't serve unless others recognize our authority?

Serving is a privilege. Stepping up is a matter of understanding that we serve people because we love them. We love them because we love God. We serve God because we love Him—not because we're afraid or obligated. What you focus on is what you become! So focus on God's love. Focus on his Word. You'll become what you think about all day long. Your thoughts forecast your future. What's on your mind right now, at this moment? Become aware of what floats in the current of your thoughts on a regular basis.

A steady diet of negativity will indelibly leave you deflated, distressed, and disappointed. You end up feeling powerless—even hopeless—if such thoughts remain unchecked. Don't give up what you have by focusing on what you've lost. Focusing on your problems will keep you in defeat. The Bible says, "This book of the law shall not depart out of your mouth, but you shall meditate on it day and night that you shall observe to do accordingly all that is written in it. For then you shall have a prosperous way. Then you shall deal wisely and have good success" (Josh. 1:8 NKJV).

You have to walk by what you know and not by what you see. Negative thoughts and difficult emotions are subject to change at any given moment. If you focus on them, you will never see yourself improving. In your life, you are always going through transitions and seasons. In transition, as you step up and serve, you have to focus on what God has said, on His promises, on what is true—not on the daily conflicts and unexpected problems that try to steal your joy and hijack your peace. Focus on the positive, the eternal, the things that matter most. Anchor your attitude to Christ!

Your Next Step

1. How would you describe your attitude toward your current position of leadership service? How would your boss or supervisor describe your attitude? The people you serve?

2. What or who encourages you the most in the area where you want to continue stepping up? What positive truth—about yourself, about God, and about others—do you need to keep at the forefront of your mind each day in order to give your best?

Father, I confess that sometimes I struggle to keep my attitude positive and uplifting in the current area where I am serving. Forgive me for the times I have allowed my emotions or challenging circumstances to momentarily get the best of me. Give me Your power and patience as You remind me of my purpose in those moments. Help me to rely on Your Holy Spirit to guide me and to keep my attitude aligned on pleasing You and advancing Your kingdom. Amen.

CHAPTER EIGHT

Integrity =
Purpose + Passion

"It is true that integrity alone won't make you a leader, but without integrity you will never be one."
—Zig Ziglar

I was around eight or nine years old when I first felt called by God. As part of the children's church, or whatever we called it back then, I was often asked to read aloud that week's Bible passage. And I just couldn't help myself! Even as the words came out of my mouth, they went deep into my heart. That Scripture would just come alive to me, and as soon as I would finish reading a particular passage, I would immediately begin to comment on it.

I'd be able to minister according to the Scripture with such passion. It would just naturally come out of me. Even at such a very young age, I would just elaborate on it. And everybody would say, "Young man, you're going to preach one day. You're going to be able to minister and bless so many." I wasn't preaching—just sharing how God was speaking to me through his Word that day—but it must have touched others because our leaders always let me do it.

When others praised my "preaching," I would smile and nod and think, *"But that's not what I want to do with my life. I love the Lord, but I don't want to lead a church."* I just didn't have the passion to be a pastor and make my ministry my career focus. I was just doing what came naturally to me at that age and letting others think whatever they wanted about what this revealed about my future.

My purpose had not yet caught up with my passion.

Satisfaction from Serving

✺ Deep down inside of me, though, I could sense something going on. Even in elementary school when I would have to do oral reports, I always loved to bring the story to life with my words. Even if supposedly I was just reporting on penguins or our solar system, I would make it into some kind of story, and my enthusiasm and passion for the topic would spill out. It was the same kind of oratory gift I used when reading the Scriptures at church, applied in a slightly different direction.

Then when I was around eight, my family attended a service at Elder Matthews's church. At the end, there was an altar call, a time to come forward and make a decision to invite Jesus into your life or to rededicate your life to God, and that day I knew it was time. I knew I needed to make a change inside. So I knelt at the altar and wrestled with God, wanting to open my heart to him fully and yet still struggling. I remember telling my mom that I felt like something was pulling me back and then forward. It was a struggle, a sensation of rocking, not physically but internally, and I knew something was going on.

Then a few years later when I was about ten or eleven, I heard Pastor R. W. Schambach preach in Beaumont, Texas. My family had gone to this little church for a homecoming or revival, and I was mesmerized by the authority with which this man seemed to know God. At the end of the service, he asked if anyone there felt called to ministry. He wanted them to come forward so he could lay hands on them and pray.

My legs trembled a little as I walked down to the pulpit in front of everyone, but my heart felt calm. Others lined up alongside me, and when it was my turn, I felt Pastor Schambach's big, heavy hands rest on my head. Then this warm, peaceful feeling settled over me. Looking back, I believe that moment was when the mantle of evangelist was imparted upon me. An evangelist is simply someone who goes from place to place sharing the Good News, telling others about the grace of God. Without knowing how to explain it at the time, I knew in my heart this was my calling.

At that time, I made a decision to give my life to God and to serve Him. I yielded to the pull on my life and surrendered my resistance and dedicated myself to doing whatever God wanted me to do for Him. Even at such a young age, I would help people any way that I could. I just loved encouraging them with a verse of Scripture or some truth from God's Word. I wanted to represent who God is and uplift others in any way possible, even if it was only offering a smile or an attitude of understanding.

This desire to minister with everyone I encountered was in my DNA. Maybe I inherited that gift from my mother, who was such a joyful person and never met a stranger. Or maybe I just learned what it meant to step up by watching the example she and my father set. Either way, I discovered the satisfaction that comes from serving others—even when you don't realize it at the time!

Learning to Read

When I think about stepping up to serve while I was growing up, one incident stands out in my memory. Each summer I would go stay with my mother's parents, Sam and Flo Coleman, for several weeks. Now I loved visiting my grandparents because they spoiled me, cooked for me, and fussed over me. But that summer after I had dedicated my life to God, I became frustrated. It all started when one day my grandfather asked me if I could read.

"Yes, sir," I said proudly.

"Very good, Johnny," Grandpa said. "Then prove it! Let's hear you read something—how about that letter over there on the table by your grandmother?"

Grandma smiled and handed me the letter, so I opened it and read aloud.

"Flo, did you hear that? Our Bubba sounds like a college professor! Is he smart or what!"

My grandmother agreed and praised my oratory skills with just as much enthusiasm. Based on the way the two of them reacted, you would have thought I had just recited the Gettysburg Address instead of a letter from the gas company about the new tank that would be installed that fall! Nonetheless, I soaked in their attention and didn't think much of it until the next day when we went through the entire scene again. My grandfather asked me if I could read; I said "yes," and then he had my grandmother hand me a piece of mail so I could prove it. It was like they had no memory of the exchange we had the previous day.

This happened the next day, and the next, and went on for the rest of my visit. It was beyond annoying! What did I have to do to prove to these people I could read just fine? I kept wondering if I wasn't enunciating well enough or speaking loudly enough, or if they thought I needed practice. Or maybe their minds were slipping and they actually couldn't remember. Several times I started to protest, but they seemed to enjoy it so much that I just kept going along with it, respecting my elders and trying to make them happy.

After the summer break when I returned home, my mom asked, "How did you enjoy your visit with Grandpa and Grandma? Did they spoil you rotten?"

"Yes, ma'am," I said. "I loved visiting them." And then my

face must have clouded up a bit because my mother sensed I was holding something back.

"Go on. . . ."

"Well, the only thing I didn't enjoy was that they made me prove I could read—not just once, but every day!" I described to my mother how each day we would go through the same scene as if rehearsing a play. "I never complained or talked back, but it just seemed strange to me," I told her. "I didn't like doing it over and over again—surely they could see that I could read—but I tried to be good about it."

My mother's face lit up in this million-dollar smile that became a chuckle. "Honey," she said, "Grandpa and Grandma asked you to do that every day because *they* can't read! They're embarrassed by it and wouldn't tell you, but they needed you to read their mail to them!"

When I visited the next year, I didn't wait for my grandfather to ask me to demonstrate my literacy. I volunteered to read their mail and acted like I just wanted to show them how much better I sounded. They clapped and laughed at my daily performance as I read letters from relatives, advertisements from local stores, and bills from the gas company. My grandparents never knew that I knew they could not read.

Equipped by Integrity

You never know how your simple act of kindness and obedience can bless someone else. And in the process of serving, you receive a blessing as well! In fact, that experience with reading for my grandparents taught me two important life lessons. First, never reveal or talk about someone's weakness or problem when it is not public knowledge. It can be tempting to embarrass or gain power over others, even those we love, when their weaknesses reveal themselves. But what have you really gained by emphasizing the deficiency in someone else? I suspect some people believe such emphasis highlights their own proficiency or strength when actually it only does the opposite. A bully is always weaker than the person he picks on!

The second lesson I learned is that everyone has some sort of weakness that happens to be our strength. Paul tells us, "When I am weak, then I am strong" (2 Cor. 12:10). Our strength only comes from Him, so we should think twice before we revel in our own abilities as we step up. We must remember the strength that God has given us is not just for us personally—it's so we can be strong in someone else's life.

When I went back to my grandparents' house, I gladly played along with them and didn't want to embarrass them in any way. I willingly took their teasing and accepted their attempts to hide their deficiency from me. Without realizing it at the time, I was given an opportunity to step up by serving them, just by helping them and respecting them. Through that experience, I learned that no matter what the circumstance may be, I can choose to serve.

Times may be changing, but your integrity and principles should remain the same. Your gift is what got you in the room, but your integrity is what will keep you in the room. There are really no gray areas in life. A gray area is like being lukewarm. In Revelation, God is quite clear about his response to those who are lukewarm. He instructs John to inform the church at Laodicea, "I know your deeds, that you are neither cold nor hot. I wish you were either one or the other! So, because you are lukewarm—neither hot nor cold—I am about to spit you out of my mouth" (Rev. 3:15–16).

It's all the way right or all the way wrong. Having a heart of integrity can protect you from pending danger. It can prevent you from relying on your feelings or the advice of others. Integrity reflects what is inside your heart and your willingness to act consistently based on your convictions. Integrity equips you to step up and serve—or to walk away.

Tested by Tough Times

If you look up *integrity* in most dictionaries, you'll find two meanings contained in this powerful word. First, integrity reflects a person's moral stability, the strength of their convictions, and the regular practice of living out their beliefs. But integrity also refers to being whole and undivided, being consistent and anchored by truth, not shifting every time the cultural winds change.

Consider Sam Walton, the great businessman and founder of Walmart, who opened his first retail store in the little town of Newport, Arkansas. Mr. Walton's dream to have the best general merchandise store anywhere had already taken root.

He had a gift for running a retail business and the passion to make his dream a reality. And Sam Walton's first store, a Ben Franklin variety store franchise, succeeded beyond anyone else's expectations—in fact, it did so well that Walton lost it.

Apparently the five-year lease he had signed with his landlord, the Butler Brothers, did not include a renewal option of any kind. Such options were standard in most business leases, and Walton had not thought to check for such a clause in their contract. He had made a huge mistake—and as a result, he was to be punished for his hard work and incredible success. The Butlers let Walton do all the work and, against all odds, create a thriving retail store and then pushed him out.

But Sam Walton did not let this early failure destroy him or change his commitment to his dream. Although he could have blamed himself, become bitter about the unfairness of life, and accepted his defeat, he instead used it to fuel his ultimate success. Sam Walton took what he had learned and moved to another small town nearby, Bentonville, Arkansas, which today we now know as the international headquarters for the multi-billion-dollar corporation known as Walmart. Needless to say, he never made a mistake with leases again!

But it wasn't just learning from his mistakes that made Walton successful—it was his willingness to persevere, to have confidence in his ability to start over, and to keep his faith in God. In his book *Giants of Enterprise: Seven Business Innovators and the Empires They Built*, Harvard Business School professor Richard S. Tedlow writes, "Sam Walton did not become a billionaire because he was a genius. . . . The real explanation for his success was that he had the courage of his convictions" (https://hbswk.hbs.edu/item/sam-walton-great-from-the-start). If Walton had abandoned his trust in God and allowed this setback to erode confidence in himself, then we might not know him today. Instead, however, he kept the faith and refused to be anyone other than who he was. Rather than accept defeat, he got up and found a new path toward the incredible success awaiting him.

I share this story with you because I'm convinced that the true test of our integrity occurs when we get knocked down, when others criticize us, when times get tough. Most of us experience challenging events in our lives, like Walton losing his lease, that leave us reeling and cause us to question everything we thought we knew. In these moments, our faith is tested along with our character. We may be tempted to run, to sink into the role of victim, or to find a pleasurable escape.

But people with integrity, leaders with both the personal passion and the divine purpose, refuse to give up or give in. They trust God to lift them off the ground, to help them get back on their feet, and to show them the way forward. They trust God as the source of their confidence, the glue that unites our purpose and passion to form our integrity.

Bridge of Confidence

⁂ Your confidence affects not only how you see yourself, but also how you view the world, other people, and God. I firmly believe that true confidence is spiritual in nature. Why? Because we find it mentioned in the Bible frequently. For example, Paul writes in Hebrews, "Now faith is *confidence* in what we hope for and assurance about what we do not see" (Heb. 11:1, my emphasis). The word translated here as "confidence" is *hupostasis*, which literally means the framework, the scaffold, the supporting structure, the basis for something. I think of it as the power under something that provides a foundation for what's above it.

This definition helps explain why I see confidence as being an essential quality in one's soul. Confidence in this meaning seems almost concrete. In fact, I think of the Rainbow Bridge, a huge truss-style bridge between Port Arthur and Orange on State Highway 73 east of Houston. I remember as a kid being terrified when our family would drive over this bridge. With a sharp ascent and descent over the Neches River, the Rainbow Bridge looms over twenty stories tall. It's not only the tallest bridge in Texas but has been deemed the scariest (https://www.texasstandard.org/stories/this-is-the-scariest-bridge-in-texas/). Driving on it, you feel like you're headed straight up into the sky—or else falling off the top into the water below!

As scary as that bridge is, it's been there since 1938. It has a strong supporting structure that secures it from one side to the other. Similarly, our confidence—in God and in the abilities He has given us—supports our life's journey. Our confidence is the mortar for our faith. It should build bridges in our life that last when the storms of life come and blow against us.

In addition to Paul's mention in Hebrews, we find many other references to confidence throughout the Bible (emphasis mine):

- For you have been my hope, Sovereign LORD, my *confidence* since my youth. (Psalm 71:5)
- But blessed is the one who trusts in the LORD, whose *confidence* is in him. (Jeremiah 17:7)
- This is the *confidence* we have in approaching God: that if we ask anything according to his will, he hears us. (1 John 5:14–15)
- So do not throw away your *confidence*; it will be richly rewarded. (Hebrews 10:35)

As followers of Jesus, our confidence should be greater than anyone's. Our integrity, our wholeness, and our strength in Christ are based on this confidence. When we trust God as the source of our convictions and power, then we have a foundation that might be shaken but will not crack. But if our confidence is based on something else—our money, our achievements, our popularity—then it won't last long when times get tough and the storms come. Jesus basically used this same comparison:

Therefore everyone who hears these words of mine and puts them into practice is like a wise man who built his house on the rock. The rain came down, the streams rose, and the winds blew and beat against that house; yet it did not fall, because it had its foundation on the rock. But everyone who hears these words of mine and does not put them into practice is like a foolish man who built his house on sand. The rain came down, the streams rose, and the winds blew and beat against that house, and it fell with a great crash.

—Matthew 7:24–27

Ask yourself: What is the source of *your* confidence?
Are you building on the Rock?
Or do you feel shaky on the sand?

Curing the Crisis

❄ You only have to go online or turn on the news to know that we have a crisis of confidence and a lack of integrity in the world today. Leaders at every level, whether in business, government, or even the church, have lost their bedrock foundation of confidence in God and His Word. Instead, they rely on the approval of others, the affirmation of affluence, or the assurance of their accomplishments. Even people who seem committed to serving God sometimes aren't willing to stand strong and sacrifice their own standards for God's. I'm reminded of the rich young ruler who seems so sincere in his desire to know God:

As Jesus started on his way, a man ran up to him and fell on his knees before him. "Good teacher," he asked, "what must I do to inherit eternal life?"

"Why do you call me good?" Jesus answered. "No one is good—except God alone. You know the commandments: 'You shall not murder, you shall not commit adultery, you shall not steal, you shall not give false testimony, you shall not defraud, honor your father and mother.'"

"Teacher," he declared, "all these I have kept since I was a boy."

Jesus looked at him and loved him. "One thing you lack," he said. "Go, sell everything you have and give to the poor, and you will have treasure in heaven. Then come, follow me."

At this the man's face fell. He went away sad, because he had great wealth.

Jesus looked around and said to his disciples, "How hard it is for the rich to enter the kingdom of God!"

The disciples were amazed at his words. But Jesus said again, "Children, how hard it is to enter the kingdom of God! It is easier for a camel to go through the eye of a needle than for someone who is rich to enter the kingdom of God."

The disciples were even more amazed, and said to each other, "Who then can be saved?"

Jesus looked at them and said, "With man this is impossible, but not with God; all things are possible with God."

—Mark 10:17–27

Why do I think this young man is so sincere? For one thing, he seeks out Jesus and falls on his knees before him. Right off the bat, this young man recognizes the authority of Christ as the Son of God. For another thing, this man also knows and has kept the commandments. He's not only aware of what God has commanded, but he has obeyed the commands. Finally, however, there's one thing that this wealthy individual cannot come to terms with: giving up control and putting his confidence in God and not in his money and possessions.

Jesus asked one more thing—which was in essence *everything*—but the young man could not make such a sacrifice. Obeying Jesus' instruction was a risk he simply didn't have the confidence to take. It's easy to speculate on this man's motives. Maybe he thought, *"What will others think if I give up everything for the poor? How will I enjoy myself? How will I make life work? How will everyone know I'm important?"* Sadly enough, this young man who seemed to have everything walked away without the only thing that matters. He had the cure for his crisis of confidence right in front of him and couldn't accept the gift Jesus offered him.

If this young man had been willing to shift the basis of his confidence, if he had the integrity to do what his heart longed to do, then the outcome might have been so different. It's funny, really. We don't know the young man's name, or much of anything else about him. But one act of obedience would likely have caused his name to be recorded down through the centuries as someone who trusted God and placed his faith in Jesus Christ without reservation or limitation.

If you want to step up and serve God with all your body, heart, soul, mind, and everything you do, then you must place all your confidence in him. Jesus wants all of us with full access to all areas of our life. And because Christ loves and accepts us, we have true confidence. We're told, "Let us draw near to God with a sincere heart in full assurance of faith" (Heb. 10:22). This is the source of our integrity. And integrity is what keeps us doing the right thing even when no one else is looking or will never find out. Integrity is what gives us the determination to start again after we've fallen. Integrity helps us make the hard choices.

Integrity fuses our passion and purpose into a lightning rod for God's power!

Your Next Step

1. In this chapter, integrity is defined as the marriage of purpose and passion. How would you define integrity in your own words? When have you recently demonstrated your integrity in some way, either in a personal relationship or in a leadership role?

2. On a scale of one to ten, how much confidence do you have on most days? What is the basis of your confidence? What needs to change in order for you to have the confidence that comes from relying on God as your source?

Lord, I'm so grateful for Your calling on my life. Thank You for the many gifts and abilities You have placed inside me and the experiences in my life You have used to shape and sharpen them. Once again, I surrender my ego and ambition to You and seek only to step up and serve those around me for Your purposes, for Your glory, and for the good of Your kingdom. May Your Spirit continue to empower me, to guide me, and to keep my personal passion aligned with my divine purpose. Amen.

CHAPTER NINE

Instinct for Success

"Our instincts are the treasure map for our soul's satisfaction."
—T. D. JAKES

J ohnny, I need you to preach tomorrow."

The words sent an electric current of adrenaline racing through my body.

"Tomorrow?" I asked, as my mind worked to grasp the opportunity being presented to me. Instinctively, I knew that I could do it and do it well. But then my thoughts began churning with self-doubts as I imagined what the experience might actually be like.

"Yes, my friend," Pastor Joel said. "I thought I could shake this cold, but it's only gotten worse. I'm almost to the point of having laryngitis, and my doctor told me to take it easy. As I prayed about what to do, you were the person God brought to mind."

"Well, you know I'm honored," I said, still stalling and somewhat reluctant to jump in and accept. "And I can do it, but . . . ." More reasons why I shouldn't do it battled against the instinct in me to seize this opportunity to bless so many others.

"But what? I have such peace about this! Maybe that's why I'm not supposed to preach—just so you can!" Joel's voice grew raspy and sounded like an echo fading away.

"All services?" I asked.

He laughed and repeated my words while changing the emphasis. "All services!"

"Okay, I'll just say what I'm thinking so forgive me," I said, mustering up my courage in order to confront my fears. "You and I both know there are others you could ask who are better preachers than I am. I can name a dozen people at our church—both on staff and in the congregation—who are better speakers and more dynamic in their preaching. Or you could pick up the phone and call almost any pastor in this country and they would be here in a heartbeat, thrilled to preach at Lakewood in your pulpit tomorrow."

Pastor Joel laughed again, which led him into a fit of coughing. "I'm laughing, Johnny, because you sound like Moses! Do you hear yourself? Yes, all you said may be true but has nothing to do with my invitation. It's not just that you're my friend, my right-hand man, my fellow pastor, and brother in the Lord. It's not just that I want you to preach for me— God wants you to preach for Him!"

His words sent a shiver down my spine, and I had to smile.

"I can't argue with you—let alone with the Lord!" I said, and we both laughed.

Inspired by Instinct

❊ It's funny, because if I received a call like that now, I wouldn't hesitate, wouldn't think about it, and wouldn't begin to question it. I would simply thank Pastor Joel or whoever asked and give myself to it 110 percent. But the first time a situation like this occurred, I was scared to death! All kinds of reasons—okay, excuses—ricocheted through my mind. People will be so disappointed—they came to hear Joel and they got stuck with me. I'm not prepared—I need at least a week to pray and plan and prepare a sermon that I think would be good enough to offer to our church family. I'll end up embarrassing myself and my family and even Joel because people will wonder why he asked me.

These kinds of thoughts, however, are not instinctive. No, just the opposite—they are darts from the enemy trying to weaken my willingness to serve and my natural trust in Joel and his judgment and in the Lord. I was being called to step up! And my instincts viewed this as an opportunity to do what I knew God had made me to do in a place where He had arranged for me to do it. I simply had to overcome my fears in order to follow my divine instincts for contributing successfully to God's kingdom.

Stepping up means you constantly want to improve in being the best you can be—not for your own glory or to build up your ego. When you're committed to Jesus and being guided by the Holy Spirit, then your self-improvement is motivated by the larger call to serve others. You are only fulfilled when you empty yourself for the benefit of others! Why? Because you know your purpose and experience the joy of the Lord as you live it out and give freely to those around you.

As I have shared, I'm convinced God not only prepares us and equips us through our various experiences, but He has also designed us for His purposes before we were born. The Bible tells us, "Before I formed you in the womb I knew you, and before you were born I consecrated you; I appointed you a prophet to the nations" (Jer. 1:5 ESV). We have everything we need. It doesn't matter if we don't have the experience, the degree, the level of intelligence, the looks, or the social status we think we need to succeed. If we have the Lord, then we can rest in knowing we have more than enough for whatever we are called to accomplish in this life.

Part of God's design in us manifests through what we often think of as instinct. I'm no scientist, but I think most living creatures have a natural, instinctual sense of their purpose and how they live out that purpose. I recall watching a mourning dove build a nest with its mate in the branches of an oak tree outside our bedroom window. No one had taught those birds how to gather twigs, leaves, and grass to form a nest. As it came time for eggs to be warmed and protected, they did what God made them to do. They didn't follow a calendar but knew how long they needed to sit on their eggs.

When the shells began to crack, the parents let the chicks inside peck their way out so they would begin developing their strength. Then the mother began feeding them—by breaking down insects herself and then sharing them with her infants.

Again, like virtually all living creatures, throughout the various life stages, they knew what to do because it was what they were created to do.

Human beings are no different. We not only have physical instincts, but we also have more complex instincts based on our intellectual and emotional capabilities. We often talk about having a "gut feeling" or "personal intuition" that led us to make certain decisions. We might not be able to articulate why we felt so strongly even though it has a basis formed by all our past experiences, observations, knowledge, and wisdom. This ability to use our instincts protects us from danger and also compels us toward fulfillment by maximizing our gifts and abilities.

Usually this natural progression is called maturity. Although we don't all develop at the same speed, we're all designed to grow, improve, and mature to the fullness for which God intended. Jesus said, "I have come that they may have life, and have it to the full" (John 10:10). When we see infants, we don't expect them to walk, talk, and feed themselves. But when we see a five-year-old child, we would be alarmed if he had not mastered those basic milestones. Similarly, if we encountered a teenager who could barely read, played only with dolls, and had trouble dressing herself, we would wonder about developmental impairment. God designed us to mature and to become the fullness, the abundance, of what He instilled in us.

Just as we grow from babies into mature adults, we also see this process of instinctive development in virtually every area of leadership. The first-year cello student is not expected to lead the orchestra. The little league baseball player cannot pitch in the World Series yet. The new pastor can't build a church alone or overnight. Entrepreneurs don't begin by offering all products and services like the billion-dollar monolith they might one day become. Every oak was once an acorn!

Throughout the growth process, we measure our advancement by the milestones reached, the muscle strength gained, and the return on our investments. We look for signs of how our creation has matured and increased. Any successful business owner relies on numbers to help quantify and measure the various departments, products, and employees contributing to the growth of the enterprise. Such measurements do not tell the full story or necessarily provide a replicable formula, but they do reveal certain patterns that are fundamental to healthy growth.

If maturity is not taking place or if there is no return on the investment of our time, energy, and resources, then we are failing at a basic level. We are allowing some obstacle to get in our way—and often what blocks the path is our own fear. God expects each of us to take responsibility for what he has given us and to become stewards of our divine destiny.

The Risk of Stewardship

We can never achieve success alone, but we must do our part in order for God to empower us, bless us, and provide the rest. We must step up and do our best and not be deterred by fears, frustrations, or fantasies of what might happen. We see this important truth in one of Jesus' most famous parables, the Parable of the Talents (or Bags of Gold):

Again, it will be like a man going on a journey, who called his servants and entrusted his wealth to them. To one he gave five bags of gold, to another two bags, and to another one bag, each according to his ability. Then he went on his journey. The man who had received five bags of gold went at once and put his money to work and gained five bags more. So also, the one with two bags of gold gained two more. But the man who had received one bag went off, dug a hole in the ground and hid his master's money.

After a long time the master of those servants returned and settled accounts with them. The man who had received five bags of gold brought the other five. "Master," he said, "you entrusted me with five bags of gold. See, I have gained five more."

His master replied, "Well done, good and faithful servant! You have been faithful with a few things; I will put you in charge of many things. Come and share your master's happiness!"

The man with two bags of gold also came. "Master, he said, "you entrusted me with two bags of gold; see, I have gained two more."

His master replied, "Well done, good and faithful servant! You have been faithful with a few things; I will put you in charge of many things. Come and share your master's happiness!"

Then the man who had received one bag of gold came. "Master," he said, "I knew that you are a hard man, harvesting where you have not sown and gathering where you have not scattered seed. So I was afraid and went out and hid your gold in the ground. See, here is what belongs to you."

His master replied, "You wicked, lazy servant! So you knew that I harvest where I have not sown and gather where I have not scattered seed? Well then, you should have put my money on deposit with the bankers, so that when I returned I would have received it back with interest.

"So take the bag of gold from him and give it to the one who has ten bags. For whoever has will be given more, and they will have an abundance. Whoever does not have, even what they have will be taken from them."

—Matthew 25:14–29

Jesus makes it clear we are to use what we've been given to invest in God's kingdom. Even if and when we are afraid to take risks, he gives us the strength and courage we need to face our doubts and uncertainties. Living in fear is not an option when God has given us a divine instinct for successfully maximizing the fullness of our potential.

When we step up with humility, hard work, and dedication, then the seeds of greatness within us can take root and produce the fruit of our labor as well as the fruits of the Spirit.

We are called to risk what we have in order to produce what God wants to bring to fruition. This is the risk of stewardship.

Nonetheless, everything about this story must have shocked the audience listening to Jesus! Can you imagine what a radical idea it must have been for them to consider how someone wealthy enough to have servants would then leave them in charge of his wealth? Such a situation might be remarkable in any time and culture, but in Jesus' day, the stations of society were fixed and rarely flexible. Those born into wealth were presumed to be blessed and better than others while the poor would always struggle within their poverty and insignificance. Jesus himself once said, "The poor you will have with you always" (Mark 14:7). No one expected to move from one life station or social caste to another.

So Jesus' parable not only reinforced what it means to invest wisely as a faithful steward—it reminds us that God's kingdom functions in an entirely different economy than we know here on earth. In fact, in another parable, Jesus seemingly made this the point of his entire story, when He spoke of a landowner who hired workers for his vineyards (see Matt. 20:1–16). Although he hired different workers at different times during the day, when the master went to pay them at sundown, he paid them all the same! When one of the workers complained, the master expressed his right to pay what he wanted to whom he wanted, concluding, "So the last will be first, and the first will be last" (Matt. 20:16).

Returning to the Parable of the Talents, we might wonder why Jesus offers such a countercultural point of view. Why would servants be left in charge? Why would their master expect them to be good stewards of his wealth? While we might come up with many reasons that motivated our Savior, I suspect one of them is to inspire us to risk more! There's nothing in this parable that suggests the first two servants received special instructions, were especially brilliant, or were gifted more than anyone else. They simply did what came naturally, instinctively.

They did what they knew their master wanted them to do.

God's Gold Inside You

In the Parable of the Talents, please notice that although each servant receives a portion, they are not equally distributed. The first servant is given five bags of gold, the second one receives two bags, and the third servant gets one. Yet when the master returns, each of them must provide an account of their portion. While their amounts differed, the first two servants each doubled the master's wealth. As a result, they each receive warm words of praise from the one they serve—in fact, the same exact words of blessing and praise! He tells both of them, "Well done, good and faithful servant! You have been faithful with a few things; I will put you in charge of many things. Come and share your master's happiness!" (Matt. 25:21, 23).

Unfortunately, the third servant did not follow the example of those with whom he served. He did not double his portion—he didn't increase it at all! Arguably, we might point out that he didn't lose any of it either, but it seems that his master might have been more understanding if the servant had risked his portion and lost it than doing what he did— taking no action at all! It's almost as if the third servant is so paralyzed by fear—fear of failure, fear of uncertainty, fear of inability, on and on the list might go—that he does nothing but bury his bag of gold.

The servant even admits that he knew his master to be a shrewd businessman, "harvesting where you have not sown and gathering where you have not scattered seed" (Matt. 25:24). This admission only seems to anger his master more! The master says, "You knew this and still you buried what I had entrusted to you? You could have at least earned a little interest by putting it in the bank!" (see Matt. 25:26–27, my paraphrase). He then takes the bag of gold away and chastises this servant as "wicked" and "lazy" (Matt. 25:28), his displeasure just as evident as his pleasure had been with the first two servants.

Like the servants in this parable, we must recognize that our Master has made us stewards of His kingdom. We are not given equal amounts, but we're all given something, often more than we realize. Any time we have an opportunity—no matter where it might be, at home or at work, at school or at church—our Master expects us to make the most of it. In the parable, the master never tells the servants to make more from what he gave them—they instinctively knew to do this! Even the third servant knew this.

Our Lord holds us accountable to produce fruit from the seeds we're given. And we're not all held accountable to the same standard! The master didn't expect the second steward to produce ten bags of gold like the first one. But apparently God expects each of us to use what He gives us to the best of our ability. We don't perform to anyone else's standards, instructions, or expectations. We don't need to compare ourselves to others and feel inferior or superior.

We simply need to do all that our Creator made us to do. There are no excuses. We either take that risk of stewardship or we don't. So I must ask you, my friend, what has the Lord entrusted to you? And what are you doing with it? What return will your Master have on His investment?

Don't bury God's gold inside you!

Faithful, Fruitful, Fearless

※ Our instinct for success never relies on advice from others, pressure from our boss, the latest book we read, or even that great sermon we heard on Sunday. Our instincts for success spring forth from the uniqueness within us, the creative wellspring God instilled in us by design. When we surrender our will to his and allow his Spirit to guide us, then our instincts align with His purposes for our lives.

We can then expect more than we would ever accomplish on our own because we know that God alone is the source of our power. We can become more confident when stepping out in faith and taking risks because we know that they are part of God's plan for us, for our development, and for our benefit. We can face new opportunities knowing that we're serving as faithfully and fruitfully as possible.

God gives us an opportunity to grow with each and every new opportunity. Sometimes the growth comes from turning down what seems like an obvious door you would normally walk through. Such opportunities force us to choose between our temporary good and God's eternal great. We must remember that our viewpoint is limited by our mortal senses and temporal barriers. All the more reason to have our instincts aligned with the Holy Spirit!

From my experience, such opportunities have often appeared to be no-brainers. As I shared with you, I have faced several junctures where I could have started my own church, forged my own path, or created my own ministry. But notice that each of those items is preceded by *my*! They appealed to my ego and personal pride as well as to my desire to serve. After all, doesn't God want me to step up and stretch myself, relying on him and not my own ability? And isn't my whole point in this chapter to encourage you to take those leaps of faith and trust your Spirit-aligned instincts?

Yes, but often our hearts and minds try to override our instincts in order to gratify ourselves instead of serving God. What appears logical, rational, or inevitable often camouflages the miracle waiting to happen where you are! It has often been more challenging to practice patience by serving diligently at Lakewood than to go off on my own and start something new. But serving at Lakewood Church has stretched me, challenged me, and stimulated my personal and spiritual growth far more than anything else I could have done. It's a privilege to see the way God has blessed our ministry and allowed me to be part of something so much bigger than any of us—including Pastor Joel—could have done on our own.

So as you consider opportunities presented before you, trust that each is indeed a way to step up and to grow closer to the Lord. But also remember that every opportunity is not necessarily one to take. We only have to review the way the enemy tempted Jesus in the desert to see this truth illustrated: "Then Jesus was led by the Spirit into the wilderness to be tempted by the devil" (Matt. 4:1). It's important to realize why Jesus was there in the first place prior to facing the devil's three temptations—each one customized for Christ's unique identity as both God and man.

Notice that the Spirit did not tempt Jesus but did lead him into the wilderness. We all have opportunities when the Spirit calls us to go deeper into situations where we may feel disoriented, isolated, or unsure of our reason for being there. In such times, we may second-guess and wonder if, like Moses or Gideon, we heard the Lord correctly. Often we mistakenly believe if we're being obedient to God and following the guidance of his Holy Spirit that our path will be smooth sailing. But time and time again, we often experience just the opposite!

Consider all the trials and tribulations Paul faced as he

lived out his calling to share the good news of the Gospel with all people. He endured beatings, arrests, incarceration, shipwrecks, and snakebites! And yet, without a doubt, he knew he was obeying God and doing what the Lord had called him to do.

Then Peter, who would be killed for preaching the Gospel, tells us:

> Dear friends, do not be surprised at the fiery ordeal that has come on you to test you, as though something strange were happening to you. But rejoice inasmuch as you participate in the sufferings of Christ, so that you may be overjoyed when his glory is revealed. If you are insulted because of the name of Christ, you are blessed, for the Spirit of glory and of God rests on you.
>
> —1 Peter 4:12–14

I share all this to remind you that just because you follow the Lord's voice and trust your Spirit-tuned instincts you will not necessarily experience success the way you expect. We are called to be faithful and fruitful but also fearless! When we have God's power, we can withstand the temptations of the enemy when we find ourselves weakened in the wilderness. In these times, our instinct for success reinforces our commitment to obey God and follow his voice even if we can't understand—especially if we can't understand—His reasons.

We must also remember that our definition of success differs from the world's. God will always bless you as you store up heavenly riches for the advancement of his kingdom, but those blessings may not manifest themselves materially—or they might. Our culture puts so much emphasis on status symbols of luxury and success, but these do not reflect success in the eyes of the Lord. Success is making the most of what we're given.

And, yes, we are then often given more to steward. In Jesus' parable, the master explains, "You have been faithful with a few things; I will put you in charge of many things. For whoever has will be given more, and they will have an abundance" (Matt. 25:21, 29). But like the servants entrusted with their master's bags of gold, we are called to use our gifts in order to please our Master with an eternal return on our earthly investment.

When you are going through problems, you must remember who you are—and whose you are! People will sometime contradict what God has said about you. God always wants to take you to a greater glory or take you to a level where you see and know more of his glory. John the Baptist said, "He must increase, but I must decrease" (John 3:30).

In order for God to *increase* our lives, our fleshly desires and self-promotion must decrease. The more you allow the Holy Spirit to take control, the more you are led by the Holy Spirit. When you're Spirit-filled, you're also Spirit-led and Spirit-guided. Your instinct for success is the result of your unique gifts, experiences, and wisdom filtered through a Spirit-led lens. God has given you all you need to succeed!

Your Next Step

1. When have you been forced to rely on your instincts in order to follow God and live out your purpose? How have you experienced success for God's kingdom by following your instincts?

2. What risk is God presently asking you to take next as you step up and serve Him more fully? Where are you being called to invest your gifts for maximum return? What fears do you need to overcome in order to risk this investment?

＊

Lord, how can I thank You for all the blessings

You bestow upon me? You have given me so

much—all I need and more—and I praise You

for Your gracious generosity to me. Forgive me

for those times when I overlook the blessings

in my life. I pray that I would be truly grateful

and that my gratitude would motivate me to

share with others, reflecting and glorifying You,

the Source of all good things. Use Your Spirit,

Lord, to sharpen and hone my instincts for

success. Help me to trust that I have all I need

to fulfill the divine destiny for which You made

me. As I seek to step up, may all I do bring You

glory, praise, and honor. Amen.

＊

CHAPTER TEN

Gifted vs. Ambitious

"When ambition ends, happiness begins."
—THOMAS MERTON

Y ou're just not *ambitious* enough, Johnny."

My friend's words stung at first. I knew he intended them as constructive criticism, something that he assumed I didn't see that he recognized and felt obligated to tell me. He was someone I had known growing up. We had been close friends as young teenagers but then drifted apart as our lives pulled us in different directions. Years later, we reconnected when he visited Lakewood Church and recognized me. We made plans to grab coffee together and catch up. From there, we began getting together about once a month just to share about our lives and families, our jobs and relationship with God.

"You're so gifted," he continued. "I just think you should explore starting your own church, your own ministry. I know you're valued at Lakewood, but . . . you just don't seem to want to do more with what God has given you."

I smiled and waited a full minute or two before responding. And then I told him, "Thank you, my friend. You've paid me a great compliment by telling me I'm not ambitious enough! Because I truly believe that my personal ambition only gets in the way of serving with the gifts God has given me."

Ego-Driven or Spirit-Led?

✳ I considered my friend's observation a compliment because I believe there's a huge difference between being motivated to succeed versus being motivated to serve. Not that the two are mutually exclusive, but when you're more motivated to achieve than to step up and lead through service, then your ambition can hijack your leadership trajectory. Instead of serving where God wants you, suddenly you begin trying to climb the ladder of success fueled by your own desire to reach the top, to be over everyone else, and to prove your abilities for all to see.

Simply put, we can either be driven by our egos or led by God's Spirit.

The way I see it, being gifted by God to serve involves recognizing how he has blessed you by design and by discovery. Before you were even born, God endowed you with natural abilities, talents, and gifts. As you grow and mature in your relationship with Him, you then discover how to use those innate abilities to live out your purpose as you serve others for God's glory and for the advancement of His kingdom.

Ambition, however, drives a wedge into that process and attempts to separate your many gifts from the purposes for which God intended them. Instead of reflecting His glory and advancing His purpose, human ambition directs the glory back to us. Ambition stokes a strong, fervent desire in us to illuminate our own greatness. Our success, wealth, achievements, and fame become evidence of our ambition as well as more fuel for the bonfire of pride, vanity, and ego within us.

We all have a God-given gift to help someone and to make things better. It has to be developed over time. If a person is led only by their personal ambition, it will eventually lead to destruction. Some people may call it your special blessing, a gift, or anointing. Often we will have passion about something and have a great desire to do it. We dream about doing what we know God has called us to do and wake up thinking about how to make those dreams come true. Scripture says, "A man's gift makes room for him and brings him before the great" (Prov. 18:16 ESV).

Notice it doesn't say our *ambition* makes room for us.

Nor does it say our passion to win.

Or our desire to get ahead.

God's Word says it's our *gift* that makes room for us to step up and serve those who are great!

Your ambition, on the other hand, will cause you to think a door is open, but your gift will open the door. Why? Because

God is in our gifting and He will open doors that no one can close. When a door is open, that means you have been given permission to enter. When a door is not open, it does not mean you are at the wrong door, but perhaps the timing is not right for you to enter it. We should be still and know that it is God's timing by which we set our schedule. Sometimes we want something before we are mature enough to handle it.

Our Father knows what's best and prioritizes our development. When a child matures into adolescence, they think they're ready for adulthood without preparation. Consider the way so many teenagers can't wait to drive a car. They may know the basics, but they lack the real know-how that can only come from experience. If you give them the keys to your car before they have developed the maturity and necessary skill behind the wheel, then you endanger their life and the lives of other.

Sometimes God doesn't give us the keys to His kingdom yet simply because we're not ready. Sometimes a closed door simply means something inside of you must be developed before you can enter the room. Your gift will always follow with great peace. Ambition is driven by emotions and feeling. Gifting is empowered by God's Spirit in you.

One of the major ways to unlock your gifts is through serving. Usually you will be drawn to someone already exercising similar gifts to your own. Often birds of a feather really do flock together! People with similar gifts are often drawn to each other with the same sense of kinship and kindred spirits. Working with a person who has the same or similar gift will cause you to grow and mature. Iron sharpens iron. You gleam so much by just being around that individual.

As a young boy, being around my dad unlocked my mechanical gift to build things. Even before I knew my dad was a builder, I would start to construct things in the backyard at very young age. I also loved encouraging people, so when I was around Pastor John Osteen, my gift of encouragement was unlocked.

A true gift you will share whether you are paid or not. We all have something to offer the world that can serve as a blessing to many. We just have to release it. The more you use and exercise your gifts, the stronger they become. The enemy does not fight you for nothing, so you must have something of great value that the enemy wants. Don't give him a foothold within your ego! Don't allow your ambitions to take you away from God's great purpose. Your gifts will fuel your purpose for life—ambition requires constant refueling of praise, achievement, and trophies in order to keep going.

Grounded by Your Gifting

❋ I find it curious that many people assume that if you're successful then you must also be ambitious. I'm convinced, though, that the people who are truly successful have never lost their grounding in the gifting God gave them. They use their gifts to serve God and accept the greater responsibility He gives them as they step up.

I see this illustrated in a question I'm often asked about Pastor Joel. You'd think after so many different people have asked the same type of question, I would expect it by now, but because of my answer to their question, I'm still amazed when someone asks me: "What's Pastor Joel *really* like? Has success gone to his head? How has he changed since Lakewood has grown so much and he's become so well known?"

Having known Joel Osteen for well over half my life now, I can say without a doubt that he is the same big-hearted, generous, positive, smart, faithful follower of Jesus that I met as a boy in a Sunday school class so many decades ago. Some people are so genuine, so transparent that you can tell who they are right away. They have no guile, no mask, and no sense of wanting to pretend to be anyone or anything else but who God made them to be. That's who Joel has always been and continues to be. What you see is what you get! He is grounded by his gifting and always puts God first in everything he does.

I understand that it's tempting to let success go to your head, though. Perhaps you've known people who struggle with staying grounded as they become more and more successful. You may even wrestle with this issue yourself. Maybe you grew up in hard times, without any luxuries and only the bare basics. Maybe your parents battled to make ends meet because they suffered illness or fought addictions. You might have been born into a large family, and there never seemed to be enough for you to have all you wanted—not enough food, not enough nice clothes like your friends wore, not enough toys or technology, and not enough money.

Like many people who lived with deprivation while growing up, maybe you vowed to yourself that you would one day overcome. You promised yourself that you would work hard, harder than anyone else in your family or your neighborhood, and you would make something of yourself. You would get your education, start your own business, or rise through the ranks in a company where you could shine. You would marry a smart, good-looking, Christian spouse, and the two of you would have your own family. You would live in a beautiful home in a good neighborhood, and your kids would have everything you never had.

Sound familiar? Perhaps you've overcome countless barriers and unexpected obstacles and achieved all your dreams and more—and yet it's not enough. There's still a sense of deprivation gnawing at your soul. You wake up in the middle of the night and wonder if you have enough money saved to endure another downturn in the economy. You worry that you won't be able to send your children to the best colleges.

And you hate feeling so competitive with everyone else, always comparing yourself and your success to those around you. You don't even understand the way you feel compelled to outdo your friends and neighbors, always trying to one-up them. If they get a new car, then you get a newer luxury sedan. If they post selfies on social media while bragging about their latest trip, you rush to plan a tropical vacation better than theirs. If they go on a mission trip with others from their church, you plan to go on two.

Our consumer culture thrives on our insecurities. If you

stop and consider the hundreds, if not thousands, of advertisements, commercials, and pitches bombarding you every day, you will realize the ludicrous logic beneath what they're selling. Will you really be prettier if you use this face cream or wear this perfume? Will others rush to tell you how attractive you are if you wear this brand of clothes and this kind of shoes? Can the kind of car you drive, the designer watch you wear, or the type of toilet paper you buy really validate who you are as God's precious child?

My answer is an emphatic *no*! And when we stop and think about how we measure our success, we know that nothing we can buy, wear, drive, or post online can truly define us. But if we don't use these status symbols and cultural tokens to show others and ourselves how successful we are, then how do we live? How do we know how important we are then? How do we face the emptiness within us if not by filling it with another pair of custom Air Jordans, a new Louis Vuitton purse, the latest iPhone, or the biggest flat screen?

For so many of us, trying to measure up is a vicious cycle. Even as you continue to exhaust yourself on this treadmill of *never enough*, you can't stop. Because if you stop, then you will have to come to terms with the fear, the emptiness, and the pain of never having had enough as a child. You will have to look at who you really are beneath the designer clothes and luxury items that you use to camouflage the cry of your soul. You will have to be laid bare before God and draw your self-worth, self-confidence, and self-awareness from Christ and Christ alone. God's Word tells us, "For *all* have sinned and fall short of the glory of God, and *all* are justified freely by his grace through the redemption that came by Christ Jesus" (Rom. 3:23–24, my emphasis).

If you let your ambitions define your drive, then you will remain on the treadmill. If you allow your God-given gifts to determine your direction, however, then you will discover the freedom of fulfilling your purpose. When people ask me how Joel remains humble, grounded, and focused on others in the midst of global success, I tell them that he never stopped putting God first—which is my goal as well. And I say goal because if we're human, I believe our enemy will always tempt us by appealing to our human ambition.

Attack on Ambition

We're not alone in our battle with personal ambition. Because He was fully human while fully God, Jesus seems to have confronted the temptations of ambition just as any other man or woman. Scripture reminds us, "For we do not have a high priest who is unable to empathize with our weaknesses, but we have one who has been tempted in every way, just as we are—yet he did not sin" (Heb. 4:15). And considering Christ had the full power of the Almighty within Him, I can't help but imagine what a persistent temptation this may have been.

In fact, this is the area the devil attacked when Jesus came out of the desert after spending forty days fasting and praying.

Satan played to the fact that Jesus didn't have to be tired, hungry, or weak as a mortal man in that moment—He could exercise His identity, power, and authority as the Son of God:

Then Jesus was led by the Spirit into the wilderness to be tempted by the devil. After fasting forty days and forty nights, he was hungry. The tempter came to him and said, "If you are the Son of God, tell these stones to become bread."

Jesus answered, "It is written: 'Man shall not live on bread alone, but on every word that comes from the mouth of God.'"

Then the devil took him to the holy city and had him stand on the highest point of the temple. "If you are the Son of God," he said, "throw yourself down. For it is written:

"'He will command his angels concerning you, and they will lift you up in their hands, so that you will not strike your foot against a stone.'"

Jesus answered him, "It is also written: 'Do not put the Lord your God to the test.'"

Again, the devil took him to a very high mountain and showed him all the kingdoms of the world and their splendor. "All this I will give you," he said, "if you will bow down and worship me."

Jesus said to him, "Away from me, Satan! For it is written: 'Worship the Lord your God, and serve him only.'"

Then the devil left him, and angels came and attended him.

—Matthew 4:1–11

Before we look at how the devil tried to appeal to the human ambition latent within Jesus, let's address how the two of them got to that point in the first place. Now it may seem strange that we're told that the Spirit led Jesus into the desert to be tempted by the devil (verse 1). Such a notion would seem to contradict the way Jesus himself instructed us to pray: "Lead us not into temptation," which we find in the Lord's Prayer (Matt. 6). But the more we compare these two ideas, the more I believe we can see their difference is not a contradiction.

God wants us to become holy in the likeness of his perfect Son. As a result, our Father never promises us that we won't be tempted or tested—only that He will never leave us or forsake us (see Deut. 31:6, Heb. 13:5) and that we will never be left defenseless. God's Word assures us, "No temptation has overtaken you except what is common to mankind. And God is faithful; he will not let you be tempted beyond what you can bear. But when you are tempted, he will also provide a way out so that you can endure it" (1 Cor. 10:13).

Based on these truths about temptation, I encourage you to remember that we can expect to be tempted, just as Jesus himself was tempted, to put ourselves and our ambition above others. We have no right to demand that God remove us from difficult situations involving temptations. In fact, the more responsibility we're given as we step up, the more we can expect to be tempted by the power and authority we wield. Serving with our gifts, we carry within us the power to accomplish great things for God's kingdom. But we also may want to abuse our power in order to make ourselves feel important, superior, or confident.

Let's keep in mind the timing and context of when the devil tempted Jesus: right after Christ had been baptized by his cousin, John the Baptist (see Matt. 3). When Jesus emerged from the baptismal waters of the Jordan River, he heard his Father's voice say, "This is my beloved Son, in whom I am well-pleased" (Matt. 3:17). From that high point, Jesus went to the desert, fasted and prayed, and then found the devil waiting to tempt him. Christ went from a high point that initiated his public ministry to a low point challenging his personal integrity.

We often face what we encounter as extreme highs and lows as well. Our greatest struggles with ambition usually occur after we have experienced a mountaintop encounter with the Lord. When I preach my best sermons and everyone goes out of their way to compliment me and tell me how much it blessed them, I feel good. So good that I can easily slide into taking credit myself! In those moments, I must remember that God is the One speaking through me for His glory and not my own.

When you get the promotion you've been praying for, complete the project that once overwhelmed you, experience God's healing touch in your body, and see God work through your efforts, then you can expect to struggle. The enemy knows that when we come off the mountaintop, it's easy for us to take a big fall. If the devil can fan the sparks of our ego enough so that we begin to take credit for what God is doing in us and through us, then our ambition catches fire!

Defenses for the Desert

✳ Once we accept that we will be tested and that our enemy knows how to activate our human ambition, then we can defend ourselves. How? By putting on the full armor of God's Spirit and arming ourselves with the truth of God's Word! Looking at the three temptations Jesus faced, we can recognize the same kinds of tricks the devil likes to use on us. And, more important, we can employ the same defensive strategies used by Jesus to resist the enemy. We all need defenses against the devil's attacks in the deserts of life!

As much as I enjoy a great meal, I fear that I might have never made it past the devil's first temptation. You see, he first attempts to appeal to Jesus' physical hunger, knowing that after fasting for more than a month, Christ would be famished. So he tries to do something logical enough—get Jesus to eat. "If you're really God's Son, then why don't you turn these rocks into bread so you can eat?" the devil taunts (see Matt. 4:3, my paraphrase). It's not that it would be a sin for Jesus to eat something in that moment—I believe the sin would have been for Jesus to take the bait and show off His power just to prove His identity as the Son of God.

But our Savior has nothing to prove—certainly not to Himself or the devil! Christ responds by countering that our spiritual nourishment is more important than our physical appetites. We need more than bread to live—we need our relationship with God and His Word. Jesus draws on the Hebrew

Scriptures to express this truth, indicating His knowledge of His Father's Word.

Next, Satan continues his assault on Christ's human ambition by directly attacking Jesus' identity. "If you're really God's Son, then prove it by jumping off this cliff so that angels will catch you!" the enemy challenges (see Matt. 4:6, my paraphrase). But Jesus responds that we are not to put God to such a test, once again referencing Scripture. Christ does not need to test His Father's love for Him. He knows He is His Father's beloved Son sent to be sacrificed so that all God's children could be saved and restored to relationship with their Creator.

Oh, how the enemy likes to attack our identities, especially when we're tired, hungry, and depleted! In those moments when we just want to relax, to experience comfort, to feel pleasure, to be loved, we may lose sight of Who loves us the most—so much He gave His life for us. Instead, our defenses crumble and we find ourselves taking that first drink and then another, that first hit and then another, that first illicit kiss and then another. "Don't you deserve this?" the devil tells us. "If God really loved you, would He let you feel so lonely, so afraid, so weary?" So in the moment, we forget who we are and Who we belong to.

When we remember how much God loves us and all He has done for us, however, then we return to our senses and stand firm in our true identity in Jesus Christ. We can withstand the appeal of whatever the devil throws at us to try and shake our commitment. We can remain humble and not succumb to inflating our self-pride, knowing God values us as His beloved son or daughter. We have nothing to prove and no reason to test our Father's love.

Finally, with Satan's third attempt to tempt Jesus, we see the most blatant attempt at triggering His human ego and ambition. Taking Christ to the vantage point of a high mountain, the devil offered Him the world—literally! "You see all those cities beneath us? All the homes, temples, and buildings? All the wealth and power down there? All of it can be yours! All You have to do is bow down and worship me!" the enemy whispers (see Matt. 4:8–9, my paraphrase).

Perhaps it's rare for us to realize those moments when we, too, are offered the world on a platter if we will simply compromise our faith in God. When a boss promises us a big raise if we will cut ethical corners. When we're alone and sitting across from a beautiful stranger who clearly is interested in more than just polite conversation. When we can attain wealth and material possessions if we will just put our greed and ambition before our humble service to others.

Jesus combats this final assault by commanding Satan to flee and declaring the eternal truth that we are to worship the Lord our God and him alone. Worshipping anyone or anything else is idolatry. When God gave the people of Israel the Ten Commandments, the very first two address the fact that not only is the Almighty the only God, but He is a jealous God and does not want us putting anything else before Him (see Exod. 20:3–4). When asked to identify the greatest commandment, Jesus said, "Love the Lord your God with all your heart and with all your soul and with all your mind and with all your strength" (Mark 12:31).

If we want to avoid the trap of ambition and instead serve in the power of the Lord through the gifts He has given us, then we must always put Him first.

Step Up and Shine

While Jesus' confrontation with the devil in the desert gives us a powerful example for how to overcome the temptations inherent in our human ambition, there is one other time when I believe Jesus faced the temptation of our human desire for power and success. Similar to the scene in the desert, this one also revolves around Jesus' identity and, in fact, begins when He asks his disciples, "Who do people say the Son of Man is?" (Matt. 16:13).

The disciples go through the short list of what they've heard on the streets of Jerusalem: John the Baptist, Elijah, Jeremiah, one of the other prophets. The Master then makes their discussion more personal by asking, "Who do you say I am?" (Matt. 16:15). Peter responds with the right answer, that Jesus is the long-awaited Messiah, God's Son come to earth in human form. Christ seems delighted with Peter's response and blesses him with the prophetic truth that Peter's faith is rock solid, the kind of solid rock upon which Christ's church will be built, one that can withstand the gates of Hades (see Matt. 16:18).

Then, curiously enough, after this little talk, Jesus told His disciples *not* to tell anyone—yet—that He is indeed the Messiah. Apparently, Christ wanted His followers to know what to expect in the months ahead, revealing His suffering and death—and His return to life. But this rattled His apostles, who may have assumed that the kingdom Jesus planned to establish was an earthly kingdom, one that would overthrow the Romans and restore the nation of Israel to her previous glory. So when they heard Jesus talking about the fact that He would eventually be killed by His own people, they reacted—especially Peter:

> Peter took him aside and began to rebuke him. "Never, Lord!" he said. "This shall never happen to you!"
>
> Jesus turned and said to Peter, "Get behind me, Satan! You are a stumbling block to me; you do not have in mind the concerns of God, but merely human concerns."
>
> Then Jesus said to his disciples, "Whoever wants to be my disciple must deny themselves and take up their cross and follow me. For whoever wants to save their life will lose it, but whoever loses their life for me will find it. What good will it be for someone to gain the whole world, yet forfeit their soul? Or what can anyone give in exchange for their soul? For the Son of Man is going to come in his Father's

glory with his angels, and then he will reward each person according to what they have done."

—Matthew 16:22–27

We don't know how much time passed from the first conversation, about who others said Jesus was, and this exchange with Peter. And it's certainly striking that instead of blessing Peter and telling him that his confession of Christ as the Messiah is the rock upon which His church would be built, as He did before, now Jesus compares Peter to Satan and calls him a stumbling block! What a dramatic reversal! The sharp contrast certainly gets our attention, and we can't help but wonder what prompted Jesus to offer such a sharp rebuke. Could Peter's assertion that Jesus must never suffer and die have been a temptation?

Remember, Jesus walked this earth fully human as well as fully divine. No matter how much He trusted His Father or wanted to serve humanity by dying for their sins, Jesus had to face the harsh reality of unfathomable pain. Not only would He be arrested and put to death like a common criminal, but He would be beaten, mocked, and humiliated in the process. No human being could possibly look forward to such anguish! Who wouldn't want to avoid such pain if possible?

Which might explain why Jesus asked His Father for a way out if possible. The night before Jesus died on the cross, He went with some of His disciples to the Garden of Gethsemane to pray. He told them that His soul overflowed with sorrow. Then He prayed, not once, but *twice* that He might not face what He also knew was inevitable: "My Father, if it is possible, may this cup be taken from me. Yet not as I will, but as you will" (Matt. 26:39). We're told that His anguish was so great that His sweat was like drops of blood (see Luke 22:44).

With this depth and intensity of emotional pain in mind, let's return to Jesus' rebuke of Peter. For His disciple to suggest that Christ might avoid doing what He came to earth to do was like the devil tempting Jesus all over again. I mean, think about how illogical this situation must have seemed. If Jesus was really the Son of God, then why didn't He do something in the face of those who persecuted Him and nailed Him to the cross beside common criminals?

And yet, our Lord did the hardest thing of all—He surrendered Himself for you and me. He stepped up in the ultimate way, choosing to forego His power, authority, and sovereignty as the Living God and dying in the mortal body of a thirty-three-year-old man. Thus, Jesus' response to Peter makes sense! Christ didn't want anyone encouraging Him to avoid doing what had to be done. And to make matters clearer, Jesus went on to explain the same is true for anyone who wishes to follow Him!

If you want to find your life, then you must lose it.

If you lose your life by following Jesus, then you will find it.

If you gain the whole world but lose your soul, what have you gained?

Is any title, status symbol, wealth, fame, or achievement worth the loss of your soul?

Do you want to advance by ambition or to serve by stepping up?

If you want to experience true success, then never settle for what ambition provides. Don't fall for the enemy's tricks when he tempts you. Keep your focus on God, even in the midst of life's greatest struggles. Step up and let your gifts shine so that others may see God through you!

Your Next Step

1. Day in and day out, what motivates you to serve? Do you feel comfortable allowing your gifts to determine your direction? Or do you struggle with putting God in the driver's seat, to lead you through your passions?

2. When have you felt driven by your own ambitions to succeed at any cost? What was the outcome of that experience? What did you learn about yourself from this incident? About God?

Dear Jesus, Your example constantly reminds me to serve with a quiet, confident commitment to God above anything else. Forgive me, Lord, when I run to the spotlight and take credit for what You're doing through me. The desire to put myself first may cause me to stumble at times, but I know that You empower me to defeat the snares of the enemy and to step up in faith. Thank You for dying for me and surrendering Your own will to the will of the Father. Give me strength through Your Spirit to step up, today and always. Amen.

CHAPTER ELEVEN

Traps of Success: Power, Pride, and Position

"Pride must die in you, or nothing of heaven can live in you."
—ANDREW MURRAY

I hear you're writing a book," a long-time friend said to me recently.

"Yes," I said, chuckling. "Can you believe it? Never could I have imagined it all those years ago when I was first starting out in ministry. But you just never know where the Lord will take you! I would never have presumed I have anything significant to share if not for the prompting of the Holy Spirit and the way God has opened doors for this book to happen."

"Well, don't forget to send me a copy. Remember your friends when you're a bestselling author!" he said, and we both laughed.

"Don't you worry about that," I said. "I know too well that

God is responsible for this book and any success it has—not me!"

After that exchange, I began thinking about how it's often more challenging to step up once you've reached certain heights of success.

The more you step up, though, the more God will always take you higher and higher. Your ongoing ascent won't necessarily mean climbing the corporate ladder of success or crashing through glass ceilings in your field of endeavor. In some cases, the more successfully you step up and serve, the more you remain behind the scenes, doing more but being seen less in the public eye.

As we have discussed, when you step up, you also serve up, putting others before yourself in order to fulfill your God-given purpose in service to God's kingdom. So in effect, you step up in joy and fulfillment by stepping down from any mountain of ambition you built and climbed yourself. Jesus said, "Whoever wants to become great among you must be your servant, and whoever wants to be first must be your slave—just as the Son of Man did not come to be served, but to serve, and to give his life as a ransom for many" (Matt. 20: 26–28). In other words, "So the last will be first, and the first will be last" (Matt. 20:16).

Success and advancement, however, bring new challenges. I have seen many successful men and women step up and use their gifts and allow the Lord to lead them to positions of greater and greater responsibility and authority. Most continue to remain humble, grateful, and faithful, trusting

God to use them as He sees fit. These individuals rarely display ambition and almost always allow their gifting to serve others, not themselves or their egos. I'm certainly blessed to serve with so many of these amazing servant leaders at Lakewood Church, starting at the top with our pastor.

Occasionally, however, I have known people who became more and more successful and lost sight of their dependence on God. As they became more powerful, they allowed their pride and position to impede their ability to continue stepping up. Instead of marveling at how far God had brought them, like Joseph did after becoming second in command to Pharaoh or Paul after encountering Jesus so dramatically on the road to Damascus, they lose sight of their true identity.

When so many other people depend on you, look to you for leadership, and rely on your gifting to sustain the team, business, ministry, or organization, then the pressure can be too much. You start to feel like you're indispensable. You begin assuming that your hard work, drive, and determination are what got you to the top. But that's never the case—God is the only reason you have climbed to new heights!

Running on Empty

❋ When I think about the pitfalls of success and the snares our enemy often sets for us, I recall Jesus' parable about a father and his two sons. This familiar story is often called the Parable of the Prodigal Son, but I believe it could also be called the Parable of Power, Pride, and Position. The conflict in the story might appear to be the result of interfamily dynamics and economic circumstances, but I'm convinced these problems originate within all of us, even if they manifest themselves in a variety of ways.

In the story Jesus tells (see Luke 15:11–32), a man with two sons was confronted by his younger son who asked to receive his inheritance right away. While there's no indication how this father felt about dividing his property and giving his younger son his share of the estate, I suspect we can guess. In effect, the son demanding his share right away made a statement about his priorities, in this case the fact that he valued immediate gratification over his love for his father or loyalty to his family. This son might as well have said, "Hey dad, I don't have time to wait around until you kick the bucket! I want my fair share right now—while I'm young enough to enjoy it."

This attitude reflects a sense of entitlement that would have shocked those listening to the story in Jesus' day. Sadly enough, I imagine most of us have encountered people, both young and old, who hold similar views about wanting what they consider their just deserts. They want the money, luxury, comfort, and convenience they see others enjoying without wanting to work for it, wait on it, or walk by faith to receive it.

While we might be tempted to question the father's wisdom in going ahead and giving his son the inheritance the young man demanded, in the long run, the father proved wiser than many. If one of my children insisted on my giving them their share of what I have, I would look at them like they were crazy! In fact, I'm guessing most parents would laugh at such a request and say, "That's funny, son! You think I would actually do that? Now get over yourself and get back to work."

But the father in this parable allowed his baby boy to take the money and run, likely knowing what the outcome would be. For you see, the younger son traveled to a distant country and began to party more than Prince back in 1999! This young man did not think about his future, let alone the impact his behavior was having on those around him. He simply ate, drank, and made merry until there was nothing left. The Scripture says he "squandered his wealth in wild living" (Luke 15:13).

With his money gone and no fast-money friends left to lean on, the young man found himself destitute in a foreign country in the midst of a severe famine. In order to survive, he begged a job from a local native who hired the young man to go out to the fields to feed pigs. One of the most heartbreaking verses of the Bible describes the young man's emptiness, both in his stomach and in his heart: "He longed to fill his stomach with the pods that the pigs were eating, but no one gave him anything" (Luke 15:16).

When fueled by self-entitlement, as the younger son was, we, too, end up running on empty. Because the truth is that each and every one of us is created in God's image. No matter what our age, race, education level, or income bracket, we are each deserving of the dignity and respect inherently included in our participation in the human race. The Golden Rule (see Matt. 7:12) tells us to treat others the same way we want to be treated.

When we feel entitled to more than others and attempt to take what we consider to be our fair share, we are basically saying that we deem ourselves more valuable, more important, and more worthy than anyone else. The reality is that as you step up and serve, you will often find yourself with more responsibility, resources, and rewards. But you are not entitled to those; you are simply God's steward of those gifts. God places people strong enough to be humble in key positions of leadership for that very reason—that they depend on Him enough to resist the temptations and snares that come with success. Sometimes, however, we may still stumble and find ourselves, like the prodigal son, empty and impoverished as the result of our own egos.

But our Father never lets us stay that way.

Vanquish Your Vertigo

When we stumble and succumb to snares of ego, ambition, or entitlement, we must never forget just how much our Heavenly Father loves us. He is the one who designed us, created us, and gave us life. He is the one who instilled our gifts, abilities, and talents for meaningful and significant purposes. He is the one who always waits for our return when we stray into the stratosphere of success and fall from the heights of our achievements and accomplishments.

When we experience the vertigo of looking down and growing dizzy by the heights we've reached, we must cling to the solid rock of our salvation. We did not arrive at the top by ourselves, so in order to vanquish vertigo over our victories, we must hold fast to eternal truth: "Every good and perfect gift is from above, coming down from the Father of the heavenly lights, who does not change like shifting shadows" (James 1:17). While this can be difficult to remember when you're figuratively slopping pigs and living with the consequences of your own selfishness, it's never too late to come to your senses. For that is what the prodigal son did:

When he came to his senses, he said, "How many of my father's hired servants have food to spare, and here I am starving to death! I will set out and go back to my father and say to him: Father, I have sinned against heaven and against you. I am no longer worthy to be called your son; make me like one of your hired servants." So he got up and went to his father.

But while he was still a long way off, his father saw him and was filled with compassion for him; he ran to his son, threw his arms around him and kissed him.

The son said to him, "Father, I have sinned against heaven and against you. I am no longer worthy to be called your son."

But the father said to his servants, "Quick! Bring the best robe and put it on him. Put a ring on his finger and sandals on his feet. Bring the fattened calf and kill it. Let's have a feast and celebrate. For this son of mine was dead and is alive again; he was lost and is found." So they began to celebrate.

—Luke 15:17–24

I never read or hear this part of the story without tears filling my eyes! Each of us can recall times when we woke up and realized that we had made a huge mistake by trusting our own desires instead of the Lord's guidance. It might have been when you took a job you knew wasn't right for you even though the title and salary made you feel oh so important. It could have been when you stayed in an abusive relationship or continued seeing someone you knew was pulling you away from God. Maybe it was switching churches or joining the choir or starting a new ministry—all of which are usually good endeavors, but not if you're doing it for your own glory and gratification. Regardless of what it was, you eventually end up facing the same dead end we all reach as the result of our own entitlement.

And that's when we once again hear God's voice calling us home!

Sometimes in order to step up we must stand up after we fall. We must allow God's gentle mercy and loving kindness to pull us to our feet and envelop us with His Spirit's healing embrace. We must take that first step toward home, humbled by our own folly and willing to accept responsibility for our actions.

But our Father never scolds us, shames us, or shuts us out—not even when we deserve it! He is there waiting with outstretched arms, exuberant and excited to welcome us home. He is there ready to celebrate our homecoming. The eternal party He throws for us can never compare with the earthly pleasures and luxuries we try to arrange for ourselves. The joy, peace, and fulfillment we experience from serving where God wants us to step up cannot compare to the counterfeit comforts we derive from temporary trophies.

Recognition, Reward, and Resentment

If the story of the prodigal son does not resonate with you, then perhaps the plight of his older brother might. Maybe you appreciate God as your loving Father and understand His gracious welcome to those who have strayed. But you also might feel just a little bit resentful, a tiny bit angry and jealous that others seem to be rewarded for their repentance after suffering the consequences of their entitlement.

Maybe it's difficult to join the party God throws when one of His lost sons or daughters steps up to return home because you have been serving faithfully and diligently all along. You've stepped up time and time again and no one has ever thrown a party for you. You've remained behind the scenes and served everyone around you without any reward or recognition. And yet others, who do far less than you and not half as well, seem to get the attention and approval that's rightfully yours.

Sound familiar? If so, then you're not alone, as we see in the older son's response to his little brother's return:

> Meanwhile, the older son was in the field. When he came near the house, he heard music and dancing. So he called one of the servants and asked him what was going on. "Your brother has come," he replied, "and your father has killed the fattened calf because he has him back safe and sound."
>
> The older brother became angry and refused to go in. So his father went out and pleaded with him. But he answered his father, "Look! All these years I've been slaving for you and never disobeyed your orders. Yet you never gave me even a young goat so I could celebrate with my friends. But when this son of yours who has squandered your property with prostitutes comes home, you kill the fattened calf for him!"
>
> "My son," the father said, "you are always with me, and everything I have is yours. But we had to celebrate and be glad, because this brother of yours was dead and is alive again; he was lost and is found."
>
> —Luke 15:25–32

The irony, of course, is that the older brother also felt entitled to more. If the younger brother seems foolish, selfish, and undeserving, then it's hard not to view his big brother as responsible, selfless, and quite deserving of their father's attention. But when we step up and serve, we can easily become martyrs blind to our own self-entitlement issues. While we give God credit for our position and rely on his power, we cling to our pride rooted in self-righteousness. We might never admit that we are better Christians, better leaders, or more humble (once again ironic!) than anyone else, but secretly we think so. We *know* so.

But that's the problem! Any time we fall into a mindset of merit, then we mistakenly believe that we're entitled to more from God. We're not like those other sinners who squander their gifts as they allow their entitled egos to fuel their success. But in truth, we are just as sinful and just as undeserving as anyone else. God's Word tells us, "None is righteous, no, not one; no one understands; no one seeks for God. All have turned aside; together they have become worthless; no one does good, not even one" (Rom. 3:10–12).

Many of the religious leaders of Jesus' time believed that they were closer to God than other people they considered unclean sinners. They believed that their good works, trips to the temple, and exalted position entitled them to moral, social, and spiritual superiority. But Jesus made it clear in no uncertain terms what He thought of them. He called them hypocrites, whitewashed tombs full of empty bones, dishes washed on the outside but not on the inside (see Matt. 23:27–28).

The truth is that none of us are ever worthy by our own merits. There is simply nothing we can do, achieve, or accomplish that brings us anywhere close to the holiness of the

Living God. The moment we begin thinking that our humility, hard work, and sacrifice elevate us above others is the moment we succumb to entitlement. We can point out prodigals all we want, but the truth is that at our core we are all prodigals. The Bible is undeniably clear: "For *all* have sinned and fall short of the glory of God" (Rom. 3:23, my emphasis).

Whether we relate more to the spoiled younger child or the self-righteous older one, the parable of power, pride, and position reminds us that we all have full access to God's grace, His love, and His provision. When you live in the Spirit and walk by faith, then no matter how high you climb, you will never stumble or fall.

Prodigal Process of Promotion

❋ The traps of success aren't all based in our entitlement or self-righteousness. Sometimes our lack of self-awareness hinders our ability to monitor our pride. Often we simply can't see our own weaknesses and blind spots. Often we become critical of others as a reflection of our own perfectionism and addiction to excellence. When people project their personal faults on to another individual, they're usually blind to it in their own life. They don't see that they are accusing or doing the same thing to someone else. They always try to correct and question that person regarding the very issues about which they are in denial.

But the higher we climb as we step up, we must remember

that when much is given much is required. God did not elevate you to your current heights in order for you to become more critical, more demanding, or more legalistic. In fact, just the opposite! When you have been given mercy and receive it, you tend to show mercy. A self-righteous person thinks his or her beliefs and morals are better than everyone else's. If you're quite sure the charity of others pales in comparison with yours, then you're just like the older brother all over again.

When people really go through a prodigal process of promotion—an experience that leaves them empty in order that they might return to God—it creates such an understanding and passion for others. On the other hand, self-entitlement will eventually remove you from whatever position you've attained. When you think you deserve something because you've earned it, then you set yourself up for disappointment. The arrogance of entitlement will always leave you empty.

Entitlement is often the result of compensating for what you didn't receive as a child and when you were growing up. If we felt ignored, neglected, or underappreciated, we may feel determined to claim the respect, attention, and affirmation we missed out on previously. If our parents had needs, limitations, struggles, or addictions that consumed the family's energy, then you may wrestle with receiving the unconditional love all children deserve for the rest of your life.

The hard news is that ultimately, no matter how well your parents loved you, it's not enough. The Good News of Jesus Christ, however, is that God can and does love us unconditionally! He loves us so much that He sent His Son to sacrifice Himself in order that we might be forgiven and have new life.

Blind to the Boomerang

❊ Entitlement can sneak up on you, too. I don't think of myself as entitled to anything more than anyone else. But like most complex attitudes, entitlement often has a range of expression. It might be very apparent in the ways you show a certain level of selfishness that makes other peoples' lives very hard. Or it might be more subtle, more passive-aggressive in the way you attempt to balance your own self-awareness with your self-entitlement.

This may come out as false modesty, an "aww shucks" demeanor that portrays you as not wanting others to notice the hard work you do even as you go on and on about not wanting them to notice. Other people usually catch on to this very quickly, though. What I find so amazing is that we can often spot issues in others but remain blind to our own! We refuse to see the log in our own eye while pointing out every speck we notice in someone else. When this form of blindness becomes habitual, our relationships, both personal and professional, will inevitably suffer.

You tend to feel sorry for yourself if things don't work out the way you want them to and often seek out attention in other ways. People may even call you a bully, a manipulator, an exaggerator, or a gossip because of the way you tend to use the truth to suit your best interests. You leave out important details and inflate others, whatever it takes to make you look good and to expose others' mistakes and weaknesses. You believe that you deserve happiness and go to great, and sometimes extreme, lengths to ensure your success, often at the expense of others.

Your interactions with others should ideally be a win–win for everyone involved. If you are the only one who wins at the end, then this reflects your own selfishness. When you impose unrealistic demands on your family, children, friends, and coworkers, your blindness will eventually boomerang back to you. Many successful people step up and then no longer see themselves or others clearly. Their attitude shifts, and they feel like remaining at the top, a place where God has brought them, suddenly depends on their own efforts. They become blind to their own faults until they reap the consequences—but often their blindness prevents them from seeing the boomerang until it's too late!

Want to see clearly and keep seeing clearly no matter how high you climb? Then don't expect anything from others that they cannot expect from you. It's that simple.

Pride Packs a Punch

Overcoming our own biases and the blindness of entitlement is never easy. When I consider the long-term effects of entitlement and the way it comes around to bite us again, I think about the story of Haman in the Book of Esther. Haman, likely descended from Amalekite royalty, thought he was better than others, especially the Jewish people, and therefore deserving of respect along with certain rewards. He felt slighted by Mordecai, who refused to bow down in honor of Haman, and consequently began plotting not only the death of Mordecai but all the Jewish people.

Using his connection to King Xerxes, Haman managed to pass a law mandating genocide of the Jewish people. Haman even went so far as to have a special gallows built in the public area so that when he had Mordecai hanged, everyone would see. But all did not go according to Haman's plan. It seems to me that it wasn't enough for Haman's wicked treachery to be uncovered because first he suffered the poetic justice of having to praise his enemy Mordecai. When that boomerang of self-pride comes back to you, it often packs quite a punch! At least it did for Haman, as we see here:

> When Haman entered, the king asked him, "What should be done for the man the king delights to honor?"
>
> And Haman thought to himself, "Who is there that the king would rather honor than me?" So he answered the king, "For the man the king delights to honor, have them bring a royal robe the king has worn and a horse the king has ridden, one with a royal crest placed on its head. Then let the robe and horse be entrusted to one of the king's most noble princes. Let them robe the man the king delights to honor,

and lead him on the horse through the city streets, proclaiming before him, 'This is what is done for the man the
king delights to honor!'" "Go at once," the king commanded
Haman. "Get the robe and the horse and do just as you have
suggested for Mordecai the Jew, who sits at the king's gate.
Do not neglect anything you have recommended."

So Haman got the robe and the horse. He robed Mordecai, and led him on horseback through the city streets,
proclaiming before him, "This is what is done for the man
the king delights to honor!" Afterward Mordecai returned
to the king's gate. But Haman rushed home, with his head
covered in grief, and told Zeresh his wife and all his friends
everything that had happened to him.

—Esther 6:6–12

Haman believed the king was going to honor him so he
came up with a fantasy that he expected the king to then
fulfill. Only the king, unaware of Haman's vendetta against
Mordecai, had no intention of honoring Haman. The royal
accolades not only went to Haman's enemy but Haman had to
deliver them himself!

It's downhill from there for Haman, who was not only
forced to serve the one he hated but also, in the end, suffer the
fate he had planned for his enemy. After Esther, by then Xerxes's queen, reveals Haman's plot to kill all the Jews, the king
catches Haman, desperate to plead for his life, in the queen's
room. The king is furious and orders Haman to be hanged
in the same gallows Haman intended for Mordecai, already

built and displayed in the public plaza. Talk about a serious case of "what goes around comes around"!

When you allow your own entitlement to empower your leadership, then you will punish people, give them the silent treatment, and try to verbally intimidate them when they don't do what you want them to do. You constantly see other people as competition or even as a threat. You will likely have many double standards in the way you behave and interact with other people. It might sound like: *I can be late and forget my duties and commitments, but you can't; I can treat myself to executive privileges, but you can't; I can abuse or disrespect those I lead, but you can't do the same back to me.*

Or, you may tend to *take* more than give in friendships, and the dynamics of relationships are dead giveaways to who is selfish. Perhaps you always look out for yourself, focusing on your needs and desires more than anyone else almost 100 percent of the time.

You have a hard time negotiating or compromising with others. You have a deep-seated conviction that you have priority and should always come first, even at the expense of stepping on others. You generally think that you are better, or more important, than other people and other people should see this and unquestioningly respect you. Haman struggles with all of these flaws, which eventually lead to his destruction.

Do you crave admiration and adoration from everyone around you? Do you like to assert your dominance or superiority over other people, or use your position and power to rule over people? This type of behavior reflects self-entitlement, and you have to conquer this in order for a door to open for you. Self-entitlement is a dangerous element in anyone's world. When someone says, "I deserve this" or "I deserve that," their eyes are focused on themselves and not others.

Self-entitlement will always get you off course. Like a storm generated by your own tempestuous emotions of fear, envy, jealousy, self-doubt, and inferiority, when self-entitlement controls your mind, motives, and ministry, then you will fly into turbulent winds. Soon you find yourself in a tailspin of turmoil, trapped much like Haman by your own lies, deceit, and manipulation.

Stepping up, however, will always help you stay the course and continue to go higher and higher. An exceptional person is an average individual focused on doing an exceptional job. Whatever you focus on will affect your attitude, and then your words will change. Whatever you focus on, that is what you will become. If you focus on elevating yourself while disrespecting and disparaging others, then you end up creating your own gallows, just like Haman. If you focus on serving God and honoring him every day, then your life will display the blessings. "Trust the Lord with all your heart and lean not on your own understanding: in all your ways submit to him, and he will make your paths straight" (Prov. 3:5–6).

Both the parable of the prodigal son and Haman's story remind us that self-entitlement not only limits us from being able to step up and serve the way God calls us, but it also forces us to suffer the consequences of our own selfish pride. Whatever we sow, we will reap. We should never focus on ourselves, especially at the expense of others. We should live to give, and when we live to give, we will automatically receive.

As we step up and serve God, we will experience so many unexpected blessings. The best example that currently comes to my mind is where I began this chapter: this very book. For many years, I had no desire at all to ever write a book. If I'm honest, even today my passion is not on writing a bestseller or becoming a famous author. My passion is simply to step up and serve God and everyone around me with the fullness of all God has entrusted to me in this life. I am so blessed that I simply want others to know the joy, the love, the peace, and the hope that comes from a relationship with Jesus Christ. If this book can help share that message, then I will be even more blessed by such knowledge!

Your Next Step

1. How have you recently experienced a struggle with your power, pride, or position? What seemed to trigger your struggle? Seeing others get accolades they don't deserve but you do? Feeling afraid of maintaining the level of success to which you've climbed? Something else?

2. Who or what helps you stay humble as you continue to step up? How can you maintain a balance between humility and confidence?

Dear God, I can't begin to thank You for how You continue to bless me with more growth, more responsibility, and more resources as I strive to serve You and Your kingdom. Please keep my vision focused only on You and the example of Your Son, Jesus, so that I don't begin to gaze at my own reflection and become self-absorbed. Protect me from the enemy's snares of success so that I never become entitled or assume I deserve anything more than anyone else. I surrender my pride to You, Lord, and rely on Your Holy Spirit to be the source of my power, my praise, and my purpose in this life. Amen.

CHAPTER TWELVE

Stepping Up for a Lifetime

"The key is not to prioritize what's on your schedule, but to schedule your priorities."
—STEPHEN COVEY

It can be the hardest part of my job as a pastor or the most wonderful.

Preaching someone's funeral all depends on the individual and how they lived their life. If they stepped up and served God and those around them with a loving, joyful heart, then it's a bittersweet celebration of the eternal legacy they created and left behind. We miss them and mourn them but also rejoice knowing they are fully at peace with God and no longer confined to this world but set free in heaven. We know that their hard work, dedication, and service will continue to have an impact for God's kingdom. We're left with the love, faith, and joy they brought to all the lives they touched while on this earth.

On the other hand, if the deceased individuals did not

know the Lord, did not love and serve those around them, and did not make the most of the gifts they had been given, then it's doubly sad. We mourn not only their passing and the hole they leave behind in the lives of their family, friends, and loved ones, but we also grieve the wasted potential, the lost opportunities, the missed moments when they could have stepped up and made such a difference in this world. We never judge them—that is for God and God alone to do—but we know they could have enjoyed so much more. In those services, we cling to the good memories and trust God to comfort us with His peace that passes understanding.

The older I get, the more frequently I seem to find myself in those services where we're either celebrating a homecoming or lamenting a permanent departure. Someday we will each conclude our journey of faith. But before we do, it's never too late to step up and experience the fullness God has for you. You may believe that you can't teach an old dog new tricks, but you're not a dog, my friend! You are a child of God created in His image!

Catch a Lightning Bolt

When I was a young man, I can remember feeling like time moved so slowly. I couldn't wait to get my driver's license. I couldn't wait to graduate from high school. I couldn't wait to get married. Now, however, watching my adult kids thrive and enjoying our grandkids, I feel like time slips by faster and faster. Grasping each day, each hour, each moment is like trying to catch a lightning bolt in the palm of your hand!

Whether young or old, God's Word consistently reminds us that our days are numbered and we must not take them for granted. Even when I'm not attending or preaching someone's funeral, I try to keep the words of the Psalmist as my prayer each and every day: "LORD, remind me how brief my time on earth will be. Remind me that my days are numbered, and that my life is fleeing away. My life is no longer than the width of my hand. An entire lifetime is just a moment to you; human existence is but a breath" (Ps. 39:4–5 NLT).

When I think how our days are numbered, the prophet Daniel comes to mind. It's not because of the many death-defying moments he endured, such as being in the lions' den, while being held captive in Babylon. I think of Daniel because of the way his life contrasts with the foreign kings he served in his captivity—in particular, King Belshazzar. God's interaction with this king is one of the scariest divine encounters in all of Scripture and reminds us that no one, no matter how wealthy or accomplished, can ignore the time clock ticking on their life:

> King Belshazzar gave a great banquet for a thousand of his
> nobles and drank wine with them. While Belshazzar was
> drinking his wine, he gave orders to bring in the gold and sil-
> ver goblets that Nebuchadnezzar his father had taken from
> the temple in Jerusalem, so that the king and his nobles, his

wives and his concubines might drink from them. So they brought in the gold goblets that had been taken from the temple of God in Jerusalem, and the king and his nobles, his wives and his concubines drank from them. As they drank the wine, they praised the gods of gold and silver, of bronze, iron, wood and stone. Suddenly the fingers of a human hand appeared and wrote on the plaster of the wall, near the lampstand in the royal palace. The king watched the hand as it wrote.

His face turned pale and he was so frightened that his knees knocked together and his legs gave way. The king called out for the enchanters, astrologers and diviners to be brought and said to these wise men of Babylon, "Whoever reads this writing and tells me what it means will be clothed in purple and have a gold chain placed around his neck, and he will be made the third highest ruler in the kingdom."

—Daniel 5:1–7

God Has Your Number

✳ In this scene, we couldn't ask for a better picture of what *not* to do if we want to live a meaningful life of stepping up. The first red flag I see is how Belshazzar chose to celebrate his big banquet. The problem as I see it is not that he's throwing a royal party and eating rich foods and drinking fine wines. No, the problem is that he decides to use the silver and gold goblets that Nebuchadnezzar had stolen from the temple in Jerusalem when the Babylonians conquered the Jewish people and plundered their capital. In other words, Belshazzar used sacred items from God's House as party favors for his guests— rich noblemen and their wives and their concubines.

To make matters worse, as they're toasting each other using holy Hebrew stemware, Belshazzar and his entourage started praising their idols made of gold, silver, bronze, iron, wood, and stone. Not only are they denigrating sacred items intended for worship of the one Living God, they are outright worshipping idols made out of metal, sticks, and stones! And it's at this tipping point that I suspect the Lord simply couldn't allow such blatant sinfulness to go unchecked.

Because that's when something straight out of a modern horror movie apparently happened! A human-like hand appeared out of thin air and began writing something on the wall in the royal banquet hall of the palace. Have you heard the phrase "the handwriting is on the wall"? Like many terms and phrases from the pages of Scripture, this particular one is still used today to refer to a situation where something bad is about to happen.

As if this were not scary enough, the king and his guest are unable to translate the mysterious words from some unknown language, which prompts Belshazzar to offer a major reward to anyone who can decipher the cryptic message. Cue the entrance of Daniel at this bizarre party, who warns the king that he's not going to like what the message says.

Daniel told the king that, like his father before him, Belshazzar had allowed pride to get in the way. Rather than acknowledging the sovereignty of the true God and humbling himself before the Almighty, Belshazzar did the opposite. "Instead, you have set yourself up against the Lord of heaven. You had the goblets from his temple brought to you, and you and your nobles, your wives and your concubines drank wine from them. You praised the gods of silver and gold, of bronze, iron, wood and stone, which cannot see or hear or understand. But you did not honor the God who holds in his hand your life and all your ways. Therefore he sent the hand that wrote the inscription."

—Daniel 5:23–24

Daniel then proceeds to get specific and translate the truth God had just delivered to the king. And the news does not get better! If anything, the message gets more personal as well as more intense:

Mene: God has numbered the days of your reign and brought it to an end.

Tekel: You have been weighed on the scales and found wanting.

Peres: Your kingdom is divided and given to the Medes and Persians.

—Daniel 5:26–28

While God's message hit home specifically with King Belshazzar, its relevance remains for us today. We must all remember that our days are numbered by God. Each of us will face an evaluation of how we have lived our life and used the resources that God entrusted to us as stewards during our time on earth. If we do not pursue God as our Lord and Savior, then our heart will be just as divided as Babylon when it was split by the Medes and Persians.

We may not be throwing lavish parties and flaunting idolatry like Belshazzar and his guests did. But often, we are not fully stepping up and serving. We're coasting when we should be cresting. We're resting when we should by rallying. We're settling when we should be soaring.

My friend, you don't have time to coast, rest, or settle when God has empowered and equipped you to step up! God has your number of days, and until they run out, you must continue to step up. You are called to run the good race and not grow weary. So there's no time to waste—you must keep going!

Because no matter how many days you have left, time is your most precious resource. Once we spend it, we can never get it back, never undo how we used it, never change the consequences of past decisions and actions. Money comes and goes. Relationships ebb and flow. Opportunities open and close. But time moves forward for us here on earth in a linear, progressive march through the days we have been allotted. When we take time for granted, when we literally live like there's no tomorrow, then we're making the same mistake that was ultimately Belshazzar's downfall.

Belshazzar wasted his life because he refused to see it

within the eternal perspective of eternity, the way God sees it. If he had realized this truth, then I hope he would have embraced it rather than continue living arrogantly and selfishly. With all the royal resources at his disposal, he could have stepped up and had a dramatic, positive impact on thousands of lives. As it turns out, however, he is just a tiny footnote in the pages of history, an example of what not to do, who not to be.

Surely if Belshazzar had viewed his life from an eternal perspective, then the last thing he would have chosen to do would be partying and praying to idols. And as it turns out, his story does not end well. While Daniel received the reward the king promised, time ran out for Belshazzar: "Then at Belshazzar's command, Daniel was clothed in purple, a gold chain was placed around his neck, and he was proclaimed the third highest ruler in the kingdom. That very night Belshazzar, king of the Babylonians, was slain, and Darius the Mede took over the kingdom, at the age of sixty-two" (Dan. 5:29–31). Confronted with the handwriting on the wall, this man should have realized he was at a major crossroads.

But he didn't listen.

His time ran out.

Writing Is on the Wall

❀ When you realize something is running out, you tend to value it more. When I see my bank account dip below a certain amount, I'm more careful about my spending. When I see only a few cookies left in the cookie jar, I'm only going to have one right now so that I can make the others last longer. When there are only a few minutes for an important call, I'm going to get right to the point and not waste time talking about the weather.

If we live with the perspective that our time is limited, then shouldn't we make better decisions? If you knew you only had a day, a week, a year to live, would you really want to spend several hours on social media or surfing the Internet? If you knew that you might not have much longer with a loved one, would you really want to bicker about a past grudge? If you knew that you only had a few more opportunities to serve those around you with your gifts, would you really want to withhold them?

My friend, the handwriting is on our wall, just as it was for King Belshazzar.

There's no time to waste.

What you do or don't do matters more than you realize.

Don't divide your heart, your life, or your time into fragments that keep you busy but don't accomplish anything.

If you're still reading this book right now, then you still have time to step up.

You can sharpen your focus on your priorities, the relationships that matter most, the tasks that advance God's kingdom, the goals that matter for eternity. You can use your gifts to make the world a better place. You can shine the light God has placed inside you into the darkness of a culture desperately looking for meaning. You can make a difference in someone's life this very day.

But don't put it off.

Prioritize your life so that each day counts. Live your life aligned with your faith. Don't settle for what you can accomplish in your own power when God wants to do so much through you, in you, and with you. Spend your time with people you love, people you care about, people you serve. Keep your time accountable so that you don't drift into busyness that's urgent but ultimately insignificant. Remember the words of the Psalmist: "Teach us to number our days and recognize how few they are; help us to spend them as we should" (Ps. 90:12 TLB).

Power in God's Positive

☀ If you want to spend your days as you should, if you want to step up and serve for a lifetime, then start with God's Word and return to it every day of your life. Meditate on it. Follow the Lord's instruction and obey his commandments. Begin with prayer and talk to him throughout your day. If you truly value your relationship with God more than anything else, then how can you get through your day without spending time with him?

What is your primary focus? How do you know where to begin? How can you regain your footing if you've lost your way? My answer is the same for all three questions: *focus on*

God's Word. You become what you think about all day long. What's on your mind? A steady diet of negativity will inevitably leave you deflated and stressed. It will color your decisions and prevent you from hearing God's voice. If you're always listening to the critical, complaining voice inside, it's hard to hear the whisper of God's Spirit!

But hearing God's voice is so vitally important to the decisions we make, especially ones that don't seem logical or obvious. I think about the choice my father made when I was very young and our family was growing. Dad was working for a company located in Lufkin, Texas, about a couple hours north of Houston. While he wanted to do all he could to provide for his family and give us more than he had growing up, he came to sense God prompting him to move us back to Houston. My father couldn't explain it; it's just something God placed on his heart. It was not logical because my dad was making a good living and had a promising future there in Lufkin.

Then my parents not only moved to Houston but chose to attend Lakewood Church. There were many fine churches in the area, many where our family and friends attended and wanted us to join them. Lakewood wasn't the closest one to our house or the one that we necessarily felt was the easiest for us to fit into. But Lakewood Church is the one God directed my parents to join. I fell in love with the Lord when I was ten years old, but I fell in love with serving him because we went to Lakewood. The impact that Pastors John and Dodie Osteen had on my family and me is simply incredible!

And then to be friends with their son Joel and to be blessed to minister alongside him!

All because my father chose not to stay in Lufkin, Texas.

Because he and my mother wanted us, their children, to know the Lord.

Even today, choices my parents made continue to affect my life—just like decisions I make continue to echo in the lives of my own children and grandchildren. Our choices affect everybody and everything around us. The Bible states that it's the little foxes that spoil the vine (see Song of Sol. 2:15). Similarly, I believe the little details and decisions also bring life and health to the vine of our lives. There is power in God's positive!

With most of our major decisions, we can't waste time trying to analyze, rationalize, or come up with what we think will be a "right answer." The only right answer is to trust God and seek Him first! He will direct our paths when we allow Him to guide us instead of trying to figure out things for ourselves.

Fuel for Your Focus

When you focus on the right things, it keeps your attitude positive and your attention focused on God. You don't have time to get lost in your head and lose sight of God's path for you. Paul reminds us, "Finally, brothers and sisters, whatever is true, whatever is noble, whatever is right, whatever is pure, whatever is lovely, whatever is admirable—if anything is excellent or praiseworthy—think about such things" (Phil. 4:8).

When you don't focus on the right things, you'll find yourself complaining. And if you complain, then that's where you will remain—in a state of discontent, discouragement, and disappointment. When God led the people of Israel out of bondage in Egypt, it took them forty years to reach Canaan, the Promised Land—and they complained pretty much the entire way! Bible scholars and archaeologists tell us that based on the distance between Egypt and Canaan, they could have made it there in less than a month if they had taken a direct route. When you complain and allow yourself to doubt and give in to your circumstances, however, I'm convinced it will always take longer to reach the divine destination God has for you!

When I'm tempted to complain and lose focus, I begin to count my blessings and list all the many wonderful gifts God has poured into my life. I just begin to pray and be thankful for all I have. Often people start complaining because they don't have the things in life like they planned or wanted. They won't step out in faith because they're not where they thought they would be.

I thought I'd be further along in my career at this time. I thought my marriage would be better. I thought my health would improve. I thought my children would be successful. I thought I would have saved more money.

But all this so-called thinking really only leads to complaining! And one thing I know about God is that He never responds to our complaining. He responds to our praise. So if you praise, you can't complain, but if you complain, you can't praise!

If you're complaining, then you will find yourself going in the wrong direction, but if you praise, you go to the right direction. The key is what you're focused on. Your key is what will activate something in you and keep you going through hard times.

Focusing on your deficiencies will only keep you in defeat. Focusing on your blessings is a blessing in itself! The Bible tells us just how important a steady diet of God's Word is to our overall spiritual health: "Blessed is the one who does not walk in step with the wicked or stand in the way that sinners take or sit in the company of mockers, but whose delight is in the law of the LORD, and who meditates on his law day and night" (Psalm 1:1-2, NIV).

Your Time Is Now

If you are going to step up and keep stepping up over the course of your lifetime, then you have to walk by what you know is true and not merely by what you see. The negative things in your life are subject to change at any given moment. If you focus on them, you will never see yourself improving.

You will either grow weary and want to give up, look for improvement in your own limited abilities, or seek relief by escaping into harmful habits and sinful cycles.

In life you are always going to go through transitions and seasons, which is why your stability, your security, your rock-solid foundation must be in the Lord and in His Word. When you're reeling in transition and you feel disoriented by unexpected circumstances, then you must focus on what God says. During these times you must exercise patience and wait on the Lord to reveal His direction for you.

Never make a decision when you are distressed, disappointed, or downcast. I have observed in Joel's life that he never makes a decision on anything when he has a lot on his plate or when it's the end of a busy day. He wants to make sure that he's clear minded and open to God's guidance. I've learned by his example to practice the same habit of waiting to make decisions until after I'm rested physically and refreshed by God's Word spiritually.

It's always best to wait until you're fresh to make decisions because your attitude and physical well-being always affect the way you see your life. When you are fresh, you will always make a better decision. You can think clearer, assess more comprehensively, and evaluate more effectively. Focusing on the positive outcomes while weighing the risks and potential liabilities is also essential to make informed decisions.

From there, of course, you want to spend time in prayer about the direction God wants you to take. So many people say they pray about their decisions, but when I press them about how they know God's will in their lives, many confess to me that they basically pray after they have already made their mind up. They simply want God to bless and confirm what they're already going to do. That's not the same as asking God to reveal His direction to you! You must have faith inside you before you can manifest it on the outside when the hard decisions come your way.

If you focus on how much God loves you and all that He does for you, then your perspective shifts. Suddenly those problems don't seem so big any more. Your worries don't feel so heavy. Your troubles aren't so terrible. Jesus reminds us of the power of our perspective in one of His best-known sermons: "So do not worry, saying, 'What shall we eat?' or 'What shall we drink?' or 'What shall we wear?' For the pagans run after all these things, and your heavenly Father knows that you need them. But seek first his kingdom and his righteousness, and all these things will be given to you as well" (Matt. 6:31–33).

When you're focused on God, then you'll know what to get done and what to let go. You'll stop trying so hard to make your day go the way you want it to go and instead relax in the power of the Holy Spirit within you. When you put Jesus front and center in your life, then you will get more done, get the right things done, because God's wisdom and power are so much greater than our own. I recall what Dr. King said, "The time is always right to do what is right."

Eternity is closer than you think. I pray that you live for many, many days to come, but we need to consider the reality that our days are numbered. Our human energy—physical, emotional, intellectual—is limited within our mortal bodies. No matter who we are or how important our title, job, or role, we each experience a day with only twenty-four hours, no more and no less. Don't postpone stepping up and serving with all your heart, soul, and mind until it's too late.

I know so many people who don't step up because they're waiting on the perfect conditions. They make serving others and giving all they've got conditional on other people, other factors, or other feelings. I can't tell you how many people have told me, "Pastor Johnny, I'll step up and give everything I've got once my health improves." Now, obviously, depending on one's health and physical limitations, you may not be able to move furniture or dig ditches. But what *can* you do in the midst of your illness, injury, or infirmity? Can you make a phone call, write an email, or send a text?

Others tell me variations of the same excuses. One day, after I meet the right person and get married, then I'll step up and volunteer at church. One day, after I get the right job and make more money, then I'll step up and give my time and tithes. One day, after the kids move out, then I'll step up and host a small group Bible study. One day, after my boss retires, then I'll step up and give my team 100 percent. But one day may never come, my friend!

The only day we have is today.

Don't waste time looking behind you and getting stuck in the past. And don't look so far into the future that you lose sight of what's right in front of you. The Bible emphasizes, "I tell you, *now* is the time of God's favor, *now* is the day of salvation" (2 Cor. 6:2, my emphasis).

Now is the time to step up for God.

It's not too late—yet!

With God all things are possible.

In Christ you are more than a conqueror!

This is your time—so step up!

Your Next Step

1. What consumes most of your time right now? How does the way you spend your time align with your faith and what God has called you to do? What do you need to cut from your schedule in order to realign what matters most? What do you need to add?

2. What kind of legacy do you want to leave behind when your days come to an end in this life? Who are the people you want to invest in with the rest of the time you have remaining? What needs to change in your life in order for you to step up and invest in this eternal legacy?

Dear God, I'm so grateful for the life You have given me and all the many ways You continue to bless me. Forgive me when I'm tempted to complain and overlook how You have remained faithful to me time and time again. Give me patience, Lord, when I can't see Your hand guiding me or hear Your voice leading me. I want to serve You with my whole heart and to use all the gifts that You've placed inside me. Give me strength, wisdom, and power as I trust You now more than ever, so that I may share Your love with all those around me. May I always follow the example of Jesus as a servant leader who is both strong and tender, both fierce and compassionate, and always committed to honoring his Father by putting others first. Thank You, Lord, for all I've learned through these pages. Continue to speak to me through them so that I may go out to love and serve the world! Amen.

Acknowledgments

So many friends, family, and colleagues stepped up to help me in writing this book. I could never have done it without their support and encouragement, and I appreciate each and every one of them. I thank them all for reminding me once again what stepping up is all about!

Four great men in my life have served as mentors and demonstrated a lifetime of service and leadership based on stepping up. My father, John McGowan, showed me the importance of hard work and commitment. Pastor John Osteen taught me how to invest in people, how to build a great church, and how to lead with compassion. Bishop Roy Lee Kossie always reminded me to commit everything to the Lord in prayer. Dr. Freddie Frazier instructed me with pure and simple life lessons.

Pastors Joel and Victoria Osteen, thank you for your unconditional kindness, support, and encouragement. It is a privilege to serve you and call you my pastors.

Mama Dodie Osteen, your unwavering love and kind heart is endless. To the entire Osteen family, I'm so honored to be part of an integrity-driven ministry that has so much compassion for the world and love of its people.

My good friend Paul Brady always encouraged me to write a book and invested valuable time in making it finally happen. Thank you, Paul, for pulling the material out of me and helping me find my voice.

Steven Belser and Don Iloff, thank you for your insight, wise counsel, and encouragement.

Thanks to Meleasa Houghton for opening her home so I could have a great place to write and work on this book.

Shannon Marven and Jan Miller, you are amazing. Thank you for believing in me and supporting this project. I couldn't have done it without you.

Dudley Delffs, thank you for your insight on this journey.

Thanks to Virginia and everyone at FaithWords! I appreciate your partnership more than I can express.

I'm grateful to my siblings, Deborah, Jaqueline, Regina, and Samuel. I could not ask for more awesome sisters and a wonderful brother!

Finally, thanks to Donna, Felix, Jennifer, Jonathan, Jessica, and Elizabeth. Your love and support mean everything.

About the Author

JOHNNY MCGOWAN is a man of many titles, some being armor-bearer, mentor, motivational speaker, entrepreneur, developer, and custom homebuilder. He has been a member of Lakewood Church since 1974, one of the largest nondenominational churches in America, where he currently serves as an associate pastor. Johnny offers a message of hope, servanthood, and "stepping up" to the aspiring leaders and volunteers whom he advises, as well as to pastors he ministers to on a local and global level. Johnny and his wife, Donna, share five beautiful children together and reside in Houston, Texas. www.therealjohnnymcgowan.com.